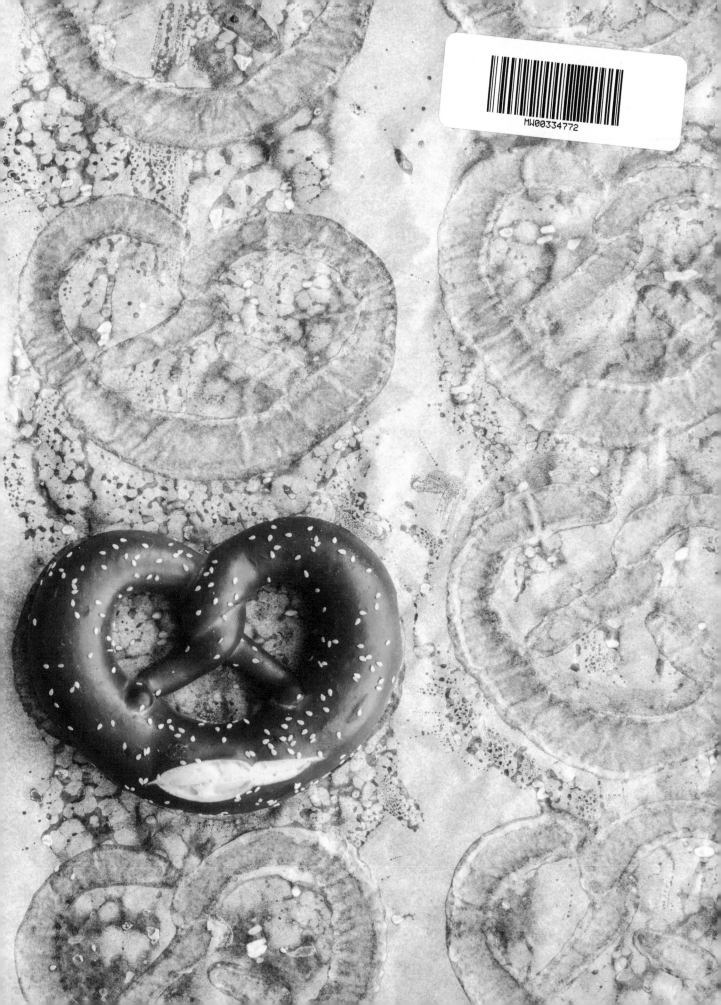

DAS COOK BOOK

GERMAN COOKING... CALIFORNIA STYLE

HANS RÖCKENWAGNER

With Jenn Garbee & Wolfgang Gussmack
Photographs by Staci Valentine

PROSPECT
·PARK·
BOOKS

PRAISE FOR
DAS COOKBOOK

"*Das Cookbook* finally gives me what I (and I think I speak for all of you) really WANT in a cookbook: bread, pastries, muesli, grilled cheese, strudel, pretzels, potatoes, and, yes, okay, salads. It's a treasure trove of ingredients and flavors combined with simple, eye-popping, tastebud-teasing recipes. Hans was classically trained and humanely raised in Germany, and he has brought it all here to California and reformulated it for an American-foodie audience. *Das Cookbook* is a modern, cool, hip take on old-school techniques and secrets. A must-have in any contemporary kitchen."

—JAMIE LEE CURTIS, actress and author

"Growing up as a chef in Los Angeles, I have always been inspired by Hans. *Das Cookbook* is just another expression of his creativity and culinary genius."

—JOSIAH CITRIN, chef/owner of Mélisse and author of *In Pursuit of Excellence*

"At a time when successful chefs take themselves much too seriously, Hans Röckenwagner has created this delectably insightful work and playfully called it *Das Cookbook*. Yet it is a serious and original blending of California and German cooking, two seemingly antithetical traditions made colorfully harmonious by a chef who is well grounded in both.

"Thus, the soft appeal of German potato salad provides just the right contrast to Korea's spicy flank steak, and the first rhubarb, straight from a local farm, gives new and rosy brightness to streuselkuchen, the much-loved crumb cake. And he shares many more recipes that modify the solidity of German food with a bright, contemporary California touch, all exquisitely illustrated and meticulously explained."

—MIMI SHERATON, former *New York Times* food critic
and author of *The German Cookbook*

CONTENTS

4. STAMMTISCH

5. SPRECHEN SIE SUPPER?

6. DAS FEST

REDISCOVERING MY CHILDHOOD CUISINE

It has been seventeen years since I wrote my first cookbook, and a lot has changed since then. I traded in the chef's whites of the high-end restaurant I owned, operated, and cooked in for twenty-three years for the civvies of a startup entrepreneur/baker. The food scene has moved from formal kitchens helmed by classically trained chefs to food trucks and pop-ups headed by unconventional culinary wizards. And once-exotic foods like kimchee and purslane are now mainstream.

Yet despite the increasing adventurousness and sophistication of the American palate, what strikes me is that German food in the United States is still misunderstood and undervalued. My publisher confirmed as much—of the many hundreds of cookbooks published each year, ones showcasing German cuisine are rare, even though Germany claims a disproportionately high number of Michelin-starred restaurants, including eleven three-stars, second only to France in Europe. And in the twenty-nine years I've lived in Los Angeles, I can count on one hand the number of German restaurants I've been to.

My hope with this book is to make German food more relatable, more approachable, and more integrated into your everyday cooking. As you will see, the recipes are meant for the home cook, and they're designed to be shared. All of these dishes mean something to me—whether it's the spätzle on the cover (the first thing I learned to make, at the age of twelve, while helping out in my parent's restaurant), or the goulash that goes so well with it (my father, a butcher, made goulash every Sunday on his day off), or the desserts (which, as the owner of a large wholesale and retail bakery, are my current obsession).

I never set out to be a crusader for German food. As I built my career as a chef in L.A., I just realized that I'd become homesick for the wealth of tastes, techniques, and flavors from my home country, and I could contribute some of that wealth to the Southern California food scene. Nothing would make me happier than the calls I'd get every spring from newly converted white asparagus lovers wondering when we were starting our white asparagus menu. Or the grateful letters I'd receive during the holidays thanking me for making authentic Christstollen. Or the many requests I still get every day from chefs, hotels, and cafés begging for our pretzel recipe.

I realize that I'm so lucky to have had the opportunity to discover new foods, cultures, and traditions in Los Angeles. What better city to learn about Mexican food, Korean barbecue, and matzo brei? What's dawning on me now—after nearly thirty years of cooking and eating in this great city—is how wonderful it has also been to rediscover the food of my German childhood. My hope is that you'll join me on this journey.

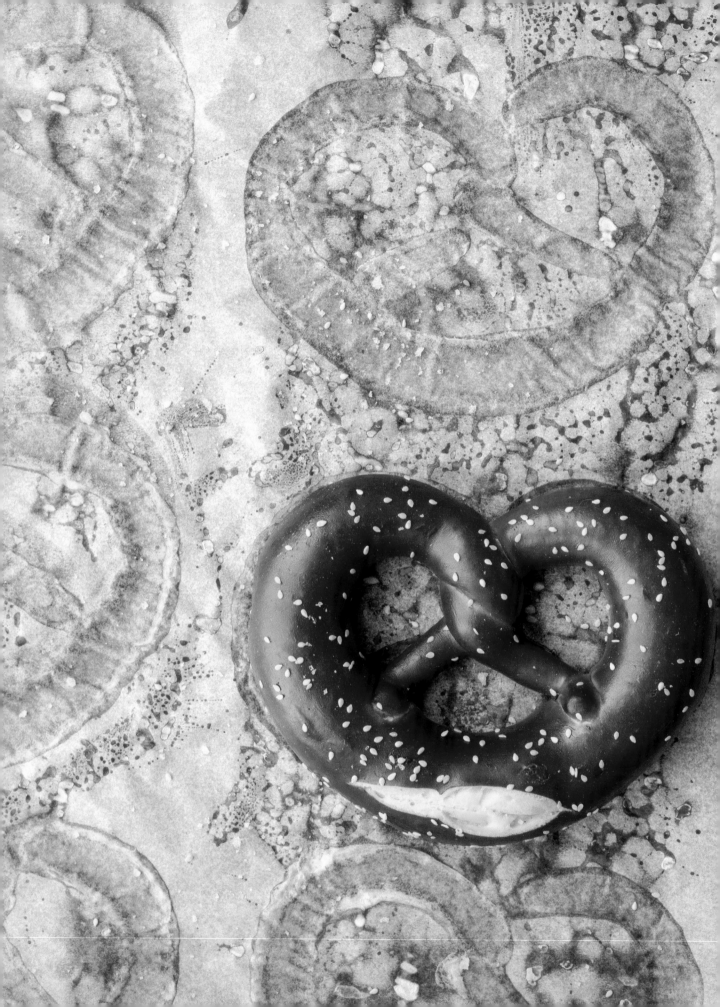

EIN

OUR DAILY BROT

THE ACCIDENTAL BAKER

I opened my first restaurant, Röckenwagner, in the 1980s, when store-bought bread almost everywhere was of pretty poor quality. Making my own bread was the only way to ensure that I'd serve a product I was proud of. To be honest, I also did it for myself, because I love to make my own breads. I started with big, fat loaves of brioche that I would slice, toast, and place in the center of every table. I wanted our guests to have a proper piece of bread to mop up their lobster sauce or simply enjoy throughout the meal. This was before buttery, French-style brioche was well known in the States, and brioche was a better complement to my style of cooking at that time than whole-grain, German-style breads. The baskets always came back empty, and pretty soon, we were baking a few extra loaves every day for our regulars to take home and freeze.

Next I began playing around with scones, and later, I moved on to the rustic German-style breads and pretzels I grew up with—after all, one can only go so long without a good pretzel. Word began to spread, and a local coffee shop called to ask if we could deliver a dozen ginger scones each morning. We'd also developed these Steiner Brot "groupies," who'd hang out around the restaurant on the days we made the famous whole-grain bread to make sure they got their weekly fix. Eventually, we opened a sliver of a bread stand at the local farmers' market. I thought a market pop-up shop once a week was all we'd ever need.

We eventually moved the restaurant to a new space with a larger kitchen, where we could set up a dedicated baking corner. It worked well for several years, and we managed to keep the face-offs between the cooks and bakers to a minimum. (Imagine trying to make dozens of loaves of bread from scratch in your home kitchen at the same time as you're prepping for an elaborate dinner party.) A few years later, when a small kitchen space with a tiny retail shop in front came up for sale, my wife, Patti, and I decided it was time to officially take the bakery leap. Back then, 1,600 square feet dedicated solely to a bakery felt like an incredible luxury. We recruited a master baker from Germany so we could meticulously work through every recipe.

As time went on, we developed more fans. I remember one day I literally had to shove the door shut with my shoulder because we had so much proofing dough in the walk-in refrigerator. It was time to either go big with baking or focus solely on our restaurants. We decided to grow the baking, and in 2010, we found our current location, a former warehouse. It seemed insanely huge, but in no time we filled it up.

Today, along with our retail bakeshops and restaurants, we sell breads and pastries to hundreds of wholesale accounts. With the business to manage, I'm no longer in the professional kitchen as much as I'd like. However, I now have an appreciation for the joys of home cooking, baking, and entertaining in a way I could never have had years ago from my perch in restaurant kitchens. This book is a compilation of some of my favorite recipes I've adapted for home cooks who want to explore the foods from my native Germany. In this chapter, the focus is on my very favorite foods of all: breads.

SOURDOUGH STARTER

In Germany, professional bakers usually have different sourdough starters, including one based on rye flour to make rye bread. At home, keeping one live starter is plenty, and really, any starter works well with whole-grain breads.

If you don't have a sourdough starter, ask around. You may find a friend who makes a mean baguette. Every time a starter is fed, some of it needs to be discarded, so home bakers are usually happy to share. If you'd rather make your own, an online search will turn up plenty of recipes. King Arthur Flour also sells a good starter online (kingarthurflour.com).

If possible, keep your starter in a ceramic crock, which allows it to breathe. A plastic storage container also works well. Just be sure to leave the lid slightly ajar. If you only bake bread occasionally (less than once a week), you can store the starter in the refrigerator so you don't have to feed it every day. It may look a little sludgy after a week in the fridge, but that's fine.

TO FEED STARTER

Feed your starter daily if you store it at room temperature; feed it weekly if you keep it in the refrigerator.

Discard ½ cup to 1 cup of starter, depending on how much you have. You want to keep at least 2 to 3 cups available for baking; more if you bake several loaves at once. Add back flour and warm/room temperature water (it should not be hot) in a 2 to 1 ratio. So, if you discarded ½ cup of starter, add back ½ cup of flour and ¼ cup of water. If you discarded 1 cup of starter, add 1 cup of flour and ½ cup of water. Stir well to incorporate.

To use refrigerated or room temperature starter, feed the starter again the night before you plan to bake. Allow the starter to rest, partially covered, at room temperature overnight. By the next day, it should be bubbly and ready to go.

The Yeast Divide

Home bread bakers tend to fall into two camps: live starter loyalists who diligently care for their sourdough starters, and those who gravitate toward the convenience and consistency of shelf-stable yeasts. I often use both in my whole-grain sourdough breads.

Beyond adding a great flavor, sourdough starters provide a solid base for a long, strong rise. Active-dry or fresh yeast (we use the latter at the bakery) gives a little extra boost to the heartier ingredients often used in German-style breads (whole-wheat and rye flours, barley, oats, nuts, and seeds), like a shot of espresso in the late afternoon. The result is a full-flavored, but lighter, whole-grain bread.

STEINER BROT

Rudolf Steiner, an early twentieth-century Austrian health-food guru, was famous for combining rye flour, honey, and water to make a bread base without any leavening agents like sourdough starter. Regardless of the purported health benefits, this whole-grain bread is an excellent combination of flavors. I use leftover bread instead of flour as the base, and add both sourdough starter and yeast (see page 11) to make a slightly lighter loaf than the original Steiner.

You can bake the bread straight away, or allow the dough to slowly rise in the refrigerator overnight. Either way, the moist bread stays fresh for several days and freezes well.

———————————— MAKES 2 LOAVES ————————————

Steiner Base

2¼ cups lukewarm water

8 ounces day-old bread, preferably a whole-grain loaf like Steiner, roughly crumbled

3 tablespoons unsalted, shelled sunflower seeds

3 tablespoons white sesame seeds

3 tablespoons whole flax seeds

⅔ cup old-fashioned oats

1 tablespoon kosher salt

2 teaspoons honey

3 tablespoons extra-virgin olive oil

Bread Dough

Steiner Base

2 cups (16 ounces) lukewarm water

2¼ teaspoons (1 package) active-dry yeast

⅓ cup plus 1 tablespoon sourdough starter, fed, at room temperature (*see page 11*)

3 cups all-purpose flour

2½ cups whole-wheat flour

½ cup rye flour (medium or dark)

½ cup wheat bran

¾ cup hazelnuts, roughly chopped

1. To make the Steiner base, combine water, crumbled bread, sunflower, sesame, and flax seeds, oats, salt, honey, and olive oil in a medium bowl. Stir to combine, cover loosely with plastic wrap, and allow to rest at room temperature at least 12 hours or overnight.

2. To make the bread dough, combine Steiner base, warm (but not hot) water, yeast, and sourdough starter in a stand mixer fitted with the paddle attachment. Mix on low speed to combine. Add all-purpose, whole-wheat, and rye flours, wheat bran, and hazelnuts. Cover mixer with a kitchen towel (to prevent flour from spilling out of bowl), and mix on low speed until ingredients come together, about 30 seconds. Switch to dough hook attachment and knead on medium-low speed for 10 minutes. Dough will be very sticky. Remove dough hook, loosely cover bowl, and allow dough to rest for 30 minutes.

3. To make the oat-seed topping, mix together sunflower seeds, sesame seeds, and oats in a small bowl.

4. Divide dough between two 1-pound loaf pans (approximately 9" x 5" or 8½" by 4½"; preferably metal, but glass also works). Roughly smooth tops, sprinkle with oat-seed topping, and press on topping lightly to adhere. Cover loosely with plastic wrap and refrigerate for 12 hours or overnight. Or, to bake immediately, leave dough uncovered and set aside in a warm spot to rise until nearly doubled, about 1 hour.

5. Thirty minutes prior to baking, preheat oven to 400°, place baking racks in middle of oven, and if dough has risen overnight, remove loaves from refrigerator and remove plastic wrap. Bake loaves, uncovered, for 25 minutes. Lower temperature to 325°, rotate pans from the front to the back of the oven, and bake until golden brown, 40 to 50 minutes longer. Total baking time is about 1 hour and 5 minutes to 1 hour and 15 minutes.

Oat-Seed Topping

2 tablespoons unsalted, shelled sunflower seeds

2 teaspoons white sesame seeds

2 tablespoons old-fashioned oats

WHOLE-GRAIN SUNFLOWER RYE

That hearty, whole-wheat-rye sunflower loaf that was all the rage in the 1970s has solid German roots. On its own or with a little cheese or jam, it's still just as good. I find myself shaving off thin slices all week.

The dough is very forgiving, but you need to allow time for it to rise three times. At the bakery, we make mini loaves. At home, one large loaf pan works well. You can cut each slice in half for smaller, cheese-worthy bites, if you'd like.

MAKES 1 LOAF

1. In a small bowl, stir together warm (it should not be hot) water, yeast, and 1 teaspoon honey. If yeast mixture does not begin to very lightly bubble (a few tiny holes should appear) after 5 minutes, discard and begin again with new yeast.

2. In the bowl of a stand mixer fitted with the dough hook attachment, combine both flours and salt. Add the yeast mixture and remaining ¼ cup honey. Mix until water is well incorporated, about 1 minute. If some flour remains at the bottom of the stand mixer, add 1 more tablespoon water and mix until incorporated.

3. Continue to knead dough on low speed until smooth, 6 to 8 minutes. Dough will be very dense. Remove stand mixer bowl, add sunflower seeds, and knead seeds into dough with your hands. Make sure sunflower seeds are well distributed; place dough on a work surface if necessary. Shape dough into a round, return to stand mixer bowl, and cover with plastic wrap or a kitchen towel. Set aside in a warm spot to rise until doubled, about 1½ to 2 hours. Punch down dough and set aside to rise again until nearly doubled, about 1 more hour.

4. Shape dough into a rectangle about 9 inches long and 4 inches wide. Lightly oil a large, deep loaf pan (preferably 9" x 5" x 2½"). Add dough, loosely cover with plastic wrap, and set aside to rise in a warm spot for 1 more hour (loaf will only slightly rise).

5. After 30 minutes, preheat oven to 350°. Bake until loaf is dark golden brown, about 1 hour (an instant-read thermometer should register about 190°). Remove bread from the oven, place on a wire rack, and allow to cool completely in the pan. To serve, thinly slice bread with a serrated knife. Slice each piece in half vertically to make smaller pieces, if desired. Store bread, tightly wrapped in plastic wrap, at room temperature for up to 5 days, refrigerate for up to 1 week, or freeze.

1½ cups (12 ounces) lukewarm water, more if needed

2¼ teaspoons (1 package) active-dry yeast

¼ cup plus 1 teaspoon honey, divided

2¾ cups whole-wheat flour

1 cup rye flour (medium or dark)

2½ teaspoons kosher salt

1 cup unsalted sunflower seeds, lightly toasted (*see page 193*)

2 to 3 teaspoons vegetable oil, for loaf pan

PRETZELS

German-style pretzels are worlds apart from doughy ballpark pretzels. I love their diverse textures, from the thick, chewy centers to the skinny, almost crispy pretzel arms. The earthy, almost sweet, and definitely salty flavor of a German pretzel is enhanced by a lye bath, so don't be tempted to leave off that step or substitute a different wash.

In Europe, the standards of flour are very consistent, but as every experienced baker bemoans, that's not the case in the U.S. It took me several years to get them just right, and I'm happy to share what I've learned.

Shaping pretzels is half the fun, so definitely let the kids help out—just be sure an adult always handles the lye wash to prevent burns (see page 17). You can find pretzel salt at many German markets and online (try americanspice.com), but coarse sea salt also works well. When it's a really hot summer, I sprinkle sesame seeds on the pretzels. When it's hot, salt tends to melt into the dough.

MAKES 8 PRETZELS

Dough

1¼ cups (10 ounces) lukewarm water

1¼ teaspoons (about ½ package) active-dry yeast

3 cups plus 2 tablespoons bread flour, divided, more for dusting

½ teaspoon kosher salt

¼ cup plus 1 tablespoon (2 ½ ounces) unsalted butter, room temperature

Lye Wash

2 tablespoons food-grade lye

Coarse pretzel, sea, or kosher salt, for sprinkling

1. In a stand mixer fitted with the dough hook, stir together warm (but not hot) water, yeast, and 2 tablespoons bread flour. If yeast mixture does not begin to bubble just a little (a few tiny holes should appear) after 5 minutes, discard and begin again with new yeast. Add remaining 3 cups flour and salt, and mix on low speed until well combined, scraping down bowl as needed. Continue to knead for 5 minutes and scrape dough off hook. Dough will be very sticky. Allow to rest, uncovered, for 5 minutes. Add softened butter and knead on low speed until dough is elastic, about 5 more minutes.

2. Lightly flour a medium bowl, add dough, and cover bowl with plastic wrap. Allow dough to rise until about doubled, about 30 minutes.

3. Lightly dust a work surface with flour and place a small bowl of water nearby. Cut dough into 8 equal pieces and roughly form each into a ball. Dip your hands in water, shake off the excess, and roll and stretch 1 ball of dough into a rope roughly 10 to 12 inches long. Set aside to rest and repeat with remaining dough.

4. Extend first rope to 18 to 20 inches and taper both ends by rolling the ends back and forth between your hands so rope is significantly wider in the middle and gradually thins (length doesn't need to be precise, and neither does the rope need to be perfectly uniform in width). Form rope into a U shape and cross approximately at the middle into an X shape. Twist one full time so you can bring both ends down to bottom of the pretzel. Gently press ends into bottom piece of dough to lightly adhere.

5. Transfer pretzels to a large, lightly floured baking sheet and use your hands to slightly expand the 3 "windows" of each pretzel. Refrigerate, uncovered, for 1 to 1½ hours.

6. Preheat oven to 400°. Place racks in top and bottom third of oven. Line 2 baking sheets with silicone-coated parchment paper or silicone mats.

7. To make lye wash, fill a large bowl with 1 quart lukewarm water. Wearing thick rubber kitchen gloves, goggles, and a long-sleeve shirt, add lye and stir occasionally until beads of lye have all dissolved, 1 minute.

8. With your gloved hands (tongs will misshape the dough), completely submerge pretzels, two at a time, in lye solution for 10 to 15 seconds (use a spatula to remove pretzels from baking sheet if necessary). Use both gloved hands to remove pretzel from the bath, gently cradling dough underneath as you lift it out. Divide pretzels among both baking sheets, arranged 2 to 3 inches apart, and use a sharp blade or knife to make a 2-inch horizontal slash in the bottom of each. Sprinkle with salt or sesame seeds and set aside at room temperature for 5 minutes to rest.

9. Bake pretzels until surface of each is shiny and dark brown, 20 to 23 minutes. Rotate pans top to bottom and front to back halfway through baking time. Cool pretzels for 10 minutes on baking sheets, peel from parchment, and enjoy warm. Allow remaining pretzels to cool completely on baking sheets. Serve the same day, or freeze for up to 2 months.

Food-Grade Lye (Sodium Hydroxide)

Commonly known as lye, food-grade sodium hydroxide is an alkali similar to baking soda that gives an authentic pretzel its telltale dark crust and almost earthy-sweet flavor.

After baking, food-grade lye is perfectly safe to eat, but it should be handled cautiously. I recommend wearing goggles, thick rubber kitchen gloves, and a long-sleeve shirt to prevent possible burns. If you don't have professional goggles, swim goggles also work well. Lye-dipped dough is very sticky, so use silicone-coated parchment paper or silicone mats on your baking sheets.

You can find food-grade lye at specialty baking shops and online at Essential Depot (www.essentialdepot.com).

STEP BY STEP: SHAPING PRETZELS

1. Extend first rope to 18 to 20 inches and taper both ends so rope is significantly wider in the middle and gradually thins.

2. Form rope into a U shape and cross approximately at the middle into an X shape.

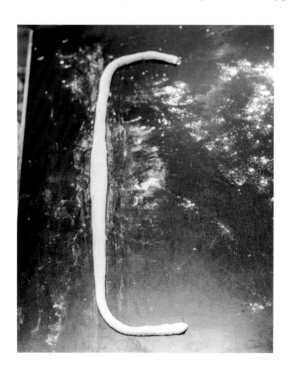

3. Twist X shape one full time.

4. Bring both ends down to bottom of the pretzel. Gently press ends into bottom piece of dough to lightly adhere. Use your hands to slightly expand the 3 "windows" of each pretzel.

PRETZEL VARIATIONS

At the bakery, I use pretzel dough as the base for everything from baguettes to whatever spirited design inspires during various holidays throughout the year. Some of my more adventurous pretzel shapes are trickier to master at home, but the ones described here are more forgiving.

HAMBURGER BUNS

Instead of forming a rope, pinch the seams together at the base of each of the 8 balls of dough and slightly flatten into a 3-inch-wide disc. Follow instructions for refrigerating and dipping buns in lye wash, let rise for 15 minutes, then follow baking instructions.

KAISER ROLLS

Twist each 10- to 12-inch rope of dough into an X shape (same as pretzels) with about 3 inches of overhang on either side at the top. Fold over and tuck the left overhang into the "hole" in the center (like a lasso), then wrap the right overhang loosely up and into the hole, so the edge rests on the side to form 3 knotlike shapes. Follow instructions for refrigerating and dipping buns in lye wash, let rise for 15 minutes, then follow baking instructions.

JALAPEÑO CHEESE PRETZELS

Shape each of the 8 balls of dough into ovals about 4 inches wide. Follow instructions for refrigerating and dipping ovals in lye wash. Immediately after dipping in lye wash, coat the back of a spoon in vegetable oil and make a wide concave indentation in the center of each dough oval. Sprinkle each oval evenly with about 3 tablespoons of sharp cheddar cheese and 3 thin slices of jalapeño. Let rise for 15 minutes, then follow baking instructions.

A DAY OR SO OLD: BREADCRUMBS

In Germany, breadcrumbs bind meatloaves, give schnitzel its signature crust, and create a nonstick base for strudel and other pastries. Home cooks also use them to "stretch" expensive ingredients like ground hazelnuts in breads and pastries by substituting breadcrumbs for part of the ground nuts.

Soft, fresh breadcrumbs work best as binders in ground meat and vegetable dishes. Toasted, finely ground breadcrumbs help develop a good crust on schnitzels and other fried dishes. Both are easy to make with day-old country-style loaves or good-quality sandwich bread, which have the right crust-to-loaf ratio and moisture content.

Sourdough breads tend to dry out very quickly and have a very thick crust, so save them for panzanella (*see recipe page 25*). Bakeries are usually happy to hand over day-old bread at a discounted price.

FRESH OR TOASTED BREADCRUMBS

Most of my recipes call for toasted breadcrumbs, but one is really just an extension of the other, so I keep both around. If your bread isn't super stale, you need to lightly toast it (step 2) to make "fresh" breadcrumbs, so they don't end up a gummy ball. Note that store-bought breadcrumbs are very finely ground and more dense than toasted, homemade breadcrumbs. If you substitute them for homemade in any of the recipes, use about half the amount.

1. Start with some day-old country-style, brioche, or good-quality sandwich bread.

2. Preheat oven to 350°. Tear bread into roughly 3-inch pieces. Scatter the bread in a single layer on rimmed baking sheets. Bake bread until lightly browned, 6 to 8 minutes, stirring once. Remove from oven and cool completely on baking sheets.

3. Process bread in a food processor in batches (do not fill processor more than half full) until finely ground, 10 to 15 seconds. Transfer to a large bowl and repeat with remaining bread. Store fresh breadcrumbs in airtight container at room temperature for up to 3 days, or freeze.

4. To make toasted breadcrumbs, preheat oven to 350°. Spread fresh breadcrumbs in an even layer no more than ¼-inch thick on a large, rimmed baking sheet. Bake until lightly toasted, 14 to 16 minutes, stirring once or twice to brown evenly. Remove from oven and cool completely. Process in batches in a food processor until finely ground. Store toasted breadcrumbs in airtight container at room temperature for up to 3 days, or freeze.

SOURDOUGH ROGGEN BROT

Roggen Brot is a specialty of the Black Forest region, where I grew up. The rustic, country-style loaf has a subtle rye flavor and the crust and chewy texture of a good sourdough. I prefer a lighter sourdough tang so as not to mask the depth of flavors in rye flour.

Loaves like this are the reason why, whenever I go out to eat at a place with great bread, I always stash a little nub by my napkin so it's safe from the servers dutifully cleaning up the table. No matter what I've had for dinner or dessert, I must end my meal with one last bite of bread.

MAKES 2 LARGE LOAVES

Starter

1 cup rye flour (medium or dark)

½ cup (4 ounces) lukewarm water

A generous ¼ cup sourdough starter, fed, at room temperature (*see page 11*)

Sponge

Starter

2¾ cups bread flour

Pinch kosher salt

1½ cups (12 ounces) lukewarm water

Olive or vegetable oil, for oiling bowl

Bread

Sponge

1 cup (8 ounces) lukewarm water

1½ teaspoons active-dry yeast (about ¾ of 1 package)

1 tablespoon extra-virgin olive or vegetable oil

2½ cups bread flour, more for flouring bowl

¾ cup rye flour (medium or dark), more for kneading

1 tablespoons plus 1 teaspoon kosher salt

1. To make the starter, mix together rye flour, warm (not hot) water, and sourdough starter in a small bowl. Cover bowl loosely with plastic wrap or a lightly dampened kitchen towel and set aside at warm room temperature for at least 3 to 4 hours, preferably overnight.

2. To make the sponge, scrape starter mixture into a stand mixer fitted with the paddle attachment. Add the bread flour, salt, and warm (not hot) water, and mix on low speed until well combined, about 1 minute. Transfer sponge to a lightly oiled medium bowl (scrape off paddle well), loosely cover with plastic wrap or a kitchen towel, and set aside at warm room temperature until doubled or more, about 1 hour.

3. To make the bread, transfer sponge mixture into a clean stand mixer bowl fitted with the dough hook attachment. Combine warm (not hot) water and yeast in a small measuring cup, stir well, and add to stand mixer along with olive or vegetable oil. Mix on low speed to roughly incorporate wet ingredients, about 30 seconds. Add bread flour, rye flour, and salt and mix on low speed until flour is gradually incorporated, about 1 minute, scraping down the bowl if needed. Continue to knead dough on low speed for 10 minutes. Dough will be very sticky.

4. Turn out dough onto a work surface generously dusted with rye flour (about ¼ cup) and shape into roughly a 12-inch square. Fold up left and right edges of dough so they meet in the center, as if you are closing the panels of a triptych. Repeat with top and bottom edges of dough so they also meet in the center. Sprinkle rye flour on top and sides of dough to cover any bare spots and flip dough upside down (dough should be lightly covered on all sides with rye flour). Set aside to rest, uncovered, for 15 minutes.

5. After 15 minutes, slightly flatten dough with your hands and repeat process of folding both the side and top edges inward and flipping the dough upside down. Dough should be noticeably less sticky. Set aside to rest for another 15 minutes.

6. Cut dough in half with a bench scraper or knife. Shape each half into a round and pinch seams together at the base of each. Cup your hands around dough and rotate it several times to form a round boule approximately 6 inches wide. Place each boule, seam-side down, in a lightly floured, 8-inch proofing basket or two lightly floured medium bowls. Place one proofing basket or bowl in the refrigerator (to slow down rise time while the other boule cooks). Allow second boule to rise at room temperature for 45 minutes to 1 hour (dough will rise significantly but may not double).

7. Preheat oven to 450° and place one rack in bottom of oven.

8. Remove second boule from refrigerator and leave to rise while you bake the first boule.

9. Place a large, heavy-bottomed Dutch oven (without lid) in the oven and heat for 10 minutes. Slash a 3-inch X across the center of the first boule with a sharp razor or knife. Remove pot from oven and carefully transfer boule, seam-side down, to it. Cover Dutch oven with its lid, return to oven, and bake for 10 minutes. Reduce temperature to 400° (do not open oven), and bake for another 10 minutes. Remove lid and continue to bake boule until top crust is a golden brown and bottom is dark brown, another 30 to 35 minutes. Total cooking time is 50 to 55 minutes. Immediately transfer bread to a wire rack to cool.

10. By now, the second boule that you chilled earlier should be ready to bake.

11. Reheat oven to 450° and carefully wipe any flour from bottom of hot pot with a damp paper towel. Preheat the Dutch oven again for 10 minutes and repeat the baking process with second boule. Cool loaves completely before slicing. Store at room temperature for 2 to 3 days or freeze.

Sourdough Roggen Brot

A DAY OR SO OLD: RYE PANZANELLA

To make a vegan version, substitute firm tofu for the feta cheese.

MAKES 3 TO 4 SERVINGS

1. Brush both sides of each slice of bread generously with olive oil. Grill, toast, or pan-sauté slices over high heat until golden brown. Tear bread into 1-inch pieces and place in a large bowl. Sprinkle salt over bread, toss well, and add cucumbers, tomatoes, green and red onions, romaine, basil, olives, and feta.

2. In a small bowl, mix together 3 tablespoons vinaigrette with lime juice. Pour over salad and toss lightly with your hands to distribute dressing. Taste and add additional salad dressing, salt, and pepper to taste. Serve immediately.

4 (1-inch) slices day-old Roggen Brot or other sourdough-rye loaf

About 2 tablespoon extra-virgin olive oil

½ teaspoon kosher salt, more to taste

2 small Persian cucumbers, sliced ¼-inch thick

2 medium heirloom tomatoes, such as Green Zebra, diced

2 green onions, white and tender green parts only, thinly sliced

½ medium red onion, halved lengthwise and thinly sliced in half moons

½ medium head romaine lettuce, sliced into 1-inch pieces

Small handful basil leaves, roughly torn

Small handful Kalamata olives, pitted and sliced in thirds (about ⅓ cup)

4 ounces (1 cup) feta cheese, crumbled

3 to 4 tablespoons Röckenwagner House Vinaigrette (*recipe page 64*), to taste

1 tablespoon lime juice

Freshly ground pepper, to taste

BRIOCHE

This is the bread that started it all for my career as a baker. The leftovers make excellent toast, both straight up with butter (as I served the bread at my first restaurant) and as french toast for breakfast.

———————— MAKES 1 LARGE LOAF ————————

⅔ cup whole milk, warmed on the stovetop or in the microwave for 15 seconds

2¼ teaspoons active-dry yeast (1 package)

⅓ cup sugar, divided

½ cup (4 ounces) unsalted butter, room temperature

3 large eggs, lightly beaten

1¼ cups all-purpose flour

2⅓ cups bread flour

½ teaspoon kosher salt

1 large egg yolk

1. Stir together warm (but not hot) milk, yeast, and 1 tablespoon sugar in a stand mixer fitted with the paddle attachment or a large bowl. If yeast mixture does not begin to very lightly bubble (a few tiny holes should appear) after 5 minutes, discard and begin again with new yeast.

2. Add remaining sugar, butter, and eggs to stand mixer or bowl. Mix on low speed until well combined, about 30 seconds (small chunks of butter will remain). If using a bowl, mix together ingredients with a large spoon. Add both flours and salt and mix on medium-low speed or with a spoon or your hands until dough comes together. Remove paddle attachment, attach dough hook, and knead on low speed until dough is smooth, 6 to 8 minutes (dough will be moist). If making by hand, butter your hands and knead dough in the bowl or on a work surface until smooth, about 8 to 10 minutes (do not add additional flour). Transfer dough to a clean bowl, cover with a kitchen towel, and set aside in a warm spot to rest for 15 minutes.

3. Reach into the bowl and knead dough with the palms of your hands until noticeably smoother, about 2 minutes. Shape dough into a rectangle about 8 inches long and 10 inches wide. Fold top and bottom edges of rectangle toward the center so they meet in the middle to form a smaller rectangle to fit in a large metal, preferably nonstick, loaf pan (9" x 5" or 8½" x 4½"). Pinch bottom seam together and place rectangle, seam-side down, in pan. Press dough evenly into pan, loosely cover dough with plastic wrap, and set aside in a warm spot to rise until nearly doubled, about 1 hour.

4. Thirty minutes prior to baking, preheat oven to 350° and place rack in middle of oven.

5. In a small bowl, whisk together egg yolk and 1 tablespoon water. Lightly brush egg wash on surface of brioche (discard excess wash). Bake for 15 minutes and reduce heat to 300°. Rotate pan front to back, and continue to bake another 35 to 40 minutes. If loaf begins to turn dark brown in the corners during the final 20 minutes, loosely tent with foil. Top should be golden brown and sound slightly hollow when tapped (an instant thermometer should read 180°). Total baking time is about 50 minutes to 55 minutes. Cool at least 30 minutes in pan. Slice and serve warm or at room temperature.

HEFEZOPF

Hefezopf is a challah-like Easter bread from southern Germany and Austria (hefe *means yeast;* zopf *is braided*). *The dough is similar to brioche, so sometimes I'll make a double batch of brioche dough and use one for this easy, three-strand loaf—instant* frühstück *(breakfast). It's traditionally made with raisins, but it's wonderful with chocolate chunks, too.*

MAKES 1 LARGE LOAF

1. Place dough on an unfloured work surface. Sprinkle chocolate or raisins on top and knead dough with palms of your hands until chocolate is well incorporated, about 2 minutes. Use a pastry cutter or knife to divide kneaded dough into 3 equal portions. Shape each portion of dough into a log about 12 inches long. Allow the strands of dough to rest for 5 minutes.

2. Place the strands of dough side by side (vertically) and pinch the top ends together so the strands are connected at the top. Braid the strands, passing the right and left strands over the middle strand like braiding hair, and pinch together the ends at the bottom. Tuck both pinched ends slightly underneath loaf.

3. Stack 2 rimmed baking sheets on top of each other and line the top pan with parchment (or use an insulated baking sheet). Transfer the braided loaf to the baking sheet, loosely cover with a kitchen towel, and allow to rise until more than doubled, 30 to 40 minutes.

4. Meanwhile, preheat oven to 350° and place rack in middle of oven. Just before baking, whisk together the egg yolk and 1 tablespoon water in a small bowl. Lightly brush egg wash on the surface of dough (discard excess wash) and sprinkle the loaf with sugar. Bake loaf until golden brown, 30 to 35 minutes. Allow to cool on baking sheet for 15 minutes and carefully transfer to a serving plate or baking rack. Serve warm or at room temperature.

Brioche dough, kneaded and risen for 15 minutes

4 ounces bittersweet or semisweet chocolate, roughly chopped, or raisins

1 large egg yolk, lightly beaten

About 2 tablespoons sugar

ROASTED TOMATO & FENNEL BREAD PUDDING

We always have plenty of day-old brioche at the bakery to make this hearty family side dish, which can also serve as a great vegetarian main course. Any slightly sweet white sandwich bread also works well.

If the bread is very fresh, leave the slices out on a sheet pan to slightly dry out overnight. If you slow-roast the tomatoes a day or two ahead, you can whip this up as a last-minute supper. And if it's summer and you can use your own (or farmers' market) tomatoes, so much the better.

MAKES 6 TO 8 SERVINGS

4 tablespoons extra-virgin olive oil, divided, more for greasing pan

1 28-ounce can whole tomatoes, drained and tomatoes sliced in half lengthwise (reserve juice for another use)

1 large clove garlic, minced

1 medium fennel bulb, stalks discarded, roughly chopped

1 cup whole milk

1 cup marinara sauce, preferably homemade (*recipe page 105*), room temperature

4 large eggs, lightly beaten

1 teaspoon fresh thyme leaves, chopped

1 teaspoon toasted fennel seeds (*see page 193*)

1 teaspoon kosher salt

1 pound (about 12 cups) day-old brioche or country-style bread, roughly chopped or torn into 1-inch pieces

⅓ cup freshly grated parmesan cheese

1. Preheat oven to 250° and place rack in bottom third of oven. Lightly rub a rectangular or square 2½- to 3-quart casserole dish (9" x 9" or 10" x 7") with olive oil.

2. Slice tomatoes in half lengthwise and scatter them on a rimmed baking sheet. Toss tomatoes with 2 tablespoons olive oil and slowly roast for 1½ hours. Tomatoes should be about half their original size but still look moist. Scatter garlic on top of tomatoes and stir with a rubber spatula to mix together well. Continue to roast tomatoes for 30 minutes, stirring occasionally (if garlic appears to be burning, remove from oven). Remove tomatoes from oven and increase temperature to 350°.

3. In a large sauté pan, heat remaining 2 tablespoons olive oil over medium-high heat. Add fennel, and sauté until crisp-tender, about 5 minutes. Set aside.

4. In a large bowl, mix together the milk, marinara, eggs, thyme, toasted fennel seeds, and salt. Add bread, fennel, and half the roasted tomatoes and mix well to combine. Transfer mixture to a baking dish and scatter remaining half of roasted tomatoes and parmesan on top. Bake until bread pudding is golden brown and firm to the touch, 40 to 45 minutes.

GUTEN MORGEN

THE MORNING MEAL

For most of us, breakfast has turned into the meal of convenience. We eat what takes the least amount of effort, and often, it's the same thing every day. That's where a little bit of planning can go a long way, like prepping Bircher Muesli the night before, so in the morning all you have to do is add a little fresh fruit.

Maybe that hurried weekday meal is why weekend brunch continues to be such a great tradition in the United States, where we have such a variety of foods. I wake up hungry, so it's not uncommon to find me in the kitchen on weekend mornings, flipping a rösti or making apple pancakes (they're always a hit) for my kids. I'm pretty sure my kids inherited the hungry-in-the-morning gene from me.

Despite my early appetite, when I first came to the States, the American-style breakfast was an adjustment. When I was growing up, the morning meal was very simple, comprising foods you might pack for a picnic: a wedge of last night's bread, maybe some ham, bologna, or other cold cuts, and always a big pot of kaffee. Probably the closest thing we had to brunch was a frühstück buffet, literally a "breakfast buffet," along the lines of what you find at those road-trip hotels in the States. Only instead of a dizzying number of cereals and a hot station packed with french toast, eggs, and sausage, you'd be greeted by neat little piles of cold cuts, sliced Emmentaler and other cheeses, maybe some chilled soft-boiled eggs, and rolls—lots and lots of fluffy breakfast rolls that you'd pull apart and stuff with the cold cuts and cheeses, and then get about your day.

The first time I saw a half-foot stack of American pancakes early in the morning, it was a little overwhelming. I was used to building up to bigger flavors and portions later in the day. You'd make a bauernomelette (farmer's omelet, an anything-goes mix of potatoes, speck, and other leftovers) for a light supper, never in the morning, and you'd definitely never serve anything sweet. Even those classic German apple pancakes, probably the longest-running brunch dish on my menus, were traditionally enjoyed after a light lunch, a sweet bite to balance a savory meal.

The longer I've lived here, the more I've come to appreciate the American-style morning meal. Things I used to eat mainly as after-school snacks, like muesli, I now keep in the fridge to grab before I head out the door. And on weekends, who doesn't love relaxing around the brunch table with family and friends, sharing bites of pancakes and omelets?

THE RÖCKENWAGNER APPLE PANCAKE

I've been making these German-style apple pancakes since I opened my first namesake restaurant in Los Angeles in the 1980s. It's not terribly time consuming, as you can prep all of the ingredients while the coffee is brewing. Still, it's something I consider a weekend project, the sort of breakfast that gives back: Everyone is happy.

When made well, German pancakes are almost like upside-down hot cakes. I mean that in the literal sense—a warm cake, not a pancake-like hotcake. We serve it in cake-like wedges so everyone can enjoy part of the crunchy crust and the soft, gooey center topped with warm caramelized apples.

MAKES 1 LARGE PANCAKE, ABOUT 4 TO 5 SERVINGS

1. Preheat oven to 350°.

2. In a small bowl, sift together flour, baking powder, and salt. In another bowl, combine cinnamon and 2 tablespoons sugar.

3. In a food processor, combine remaining ¾ cup sugar, eggs, milk, and vanilla extract and process until smooth, about 15 seconds. Add flour mixture and process again. Scrape down sides of processor, add melted butter, and blend until smooth.

4. In a large oven-proof 12-inch skillet, preferably nonstick, heat remaining 2 tablespoons butter over medium-high heat. Add apples and sauté until just beginning to brown, about 3 minutes, and reduce heat to medium. Sprinkle cinnamon-sugar on top and distribute apples evenly throughout the pan. Pour batter over apples and cook until edges are just set, about 5 to 6 minutes. Transfer pan to oven and bake until springy in center, about 15 minutes.

5. Loosen edges of pancake with rubber spatula and flip upside down onto a large serving platter so the bottom is now the top. Sprinkle with powdered sugar and top with crème fraîche or sour cream and strawberries. Serve immediately.

1 cup flour

1 teaspoon baking powder

Pinch coarse sea or kosher salt

2 teaspoons cinnamon

¾ cup plus 2 tablespoons granulated sugar

7 large eggs

½ cup whole milk

2 teaspoons vanilla extract

¼ cup (2 ounces) unsalted butter, melted, plus 2 tablespoons butter

2 medium Granny Smith apples, peeled and sliced ¼-inch thick

2 to 3 tablespoons powdered sugar, sifted, to taste

¼ cup crème fraîche or sour cream

½ pint strawberries, sliced

BUCHTELN

Buchteln are Austrian pull-apart rolls that are traditionally filled with jam, usually plum or apricot. But they've also housed poppyseed paste, squares of chocolate, and at one point in the nineteenth century, even lottery tickets.

Buchteln are typically served as dessert with vanilla cream sauce, but in the States, they're more akin to sweet rolls like those you find at brunch. If you're not an early weekend riser, you can make the dough and fill the buns the night before you bake them.

Be warned: These are addictive. Rob Long, a regular customer and neighbor at 3 Square Café in Venice, keeps asking us to install a flagpole outside and raise the flag every time we make buchteln so the locals can get some of the warm treats before they sell out.

MAKES 24 MINI SWEET ROLLS, ABOUT 8 TO 10 SERVINGS

2¼ teaspoons (1 package) active-dry yeast

1 cup whole milk, lukewarm

5 tablespoons (2½ ounces) plus 3 tablespoons (1½ ounces) unsalted butter, room temperature, plus more for bowl and pan

½ cup granulated sugar

2 large eggs

4 large egg yolks

¼ teaspoon kosher salt

4¼ cups flour, divided, plus more for dusting

About ¾ cup thick raspberry, plum, cherry, or other jam

2 tablespoons powdered sugar, sifted

1. In a small bowl, stir together yeast and warm milk (it should not be hot). Set aside for 5 minutes.

2. In the bowl of a stand mixer fitted with the paddle attachment, combine 5 tablespoons butter and ½ cup sugar. Mix on medium-low until well combined, about 1 minute. Add eggs, egg yolks, and salt, mix well, then add milk and yeast. Reduce speed to low, add 1 cup flour, and mix again. Gradually add remaining 3¼ cups flour and mix until well combined, about 1 minute, scraping down sides of bowl and paddle as needed.

3. Replace paddle with hook attachment. Reduce speed to low and knead until dough is soft, about 5 minutes. Dough will be very sticky. Butter your hands and a large bowl and transfer dough to bowl. Cover with a kitchen towel and set aside in a warm spot to rise for 30 minutes.

4. Butter your hands again, reach into bowl, and fold both sides of dough upwards toward the middle. Repeat with opposite sides, as if wrapping a package. Flip dough upside down, cover, and set aside for 15 minutes. Repeat folding process and allow dough to rest another 15 minutes. Dough should have more than doubled and be smooth enough to handle.

5. Butter a 9" x 13" glass baking dish and preheat oven to 350° (if allowing to rise overnight, do not preheat oven). Transfer dough to a lightly floured work surface. Use your hands to gently shape dough into a 12" x 12" square. With a pizza cutter or knife, cut dough into 4 equal sections vertically, then 6 equal sections horizontally to make 24 squares.

6. Slightly stretch out 1 square of dough with your fingers. Working quickly to keep dough from over-rising, place about 1 teaspoon jam in middle. Use your fingers to fold up edges and pinch them together, like a dumpling, to seal in filling. Place in baking dish, seam side down. Repeat with remaining dough, placing each round side by side.

7. Melt remaining 3 tablespoons butter and pour over rolls. Set aside to rise in a warm spot for 30 minutes. Alternatively, cover tightly with plastic wrap and refrigerate overnight.

8. If buchteln are refrigerated, remove and let sit at room temperature for 1 hour before baking. Remove plastic wrap and bake until sweet rolls are puffy and light golden brown on the top, 24 to 28 to minutes (they may take a few minutes longer if refrigerated), rotating pan front to back halfway through. Transfer to a rack to cool for 15 minutes. Dust with powdered sugar and serve immediately.

PAIN PERDU WITH ROASTED BELL PEPPERS, BACON & JALAPEÑO MAPLE SYRUP

Maybe it's my German-ness or just my family's humble background—whatever the reason, there's something extremely satisfying about not letting anything go to waste. So I've come up with a number of recipes to celebrate day-old breads. This version of french toast has a little something for everyone: savory, sweet, and spicy.

MAKE 4 SERVINGS

½ cup pure maple syrup

½ medium jalapeño, sliced in half lengthwise and seeds removed

1 tablespoon extra-virgin olive oil

4 thick (about 1¼ inches) slices day-old brioche (*recipe page 26*), or 2 brioche hamburger buns

6 large eggs, divided

1 cup whole milk

½ teaspoon coarse sea or kosher salt, more to taste

Generous pinch cayenne pepper, more to taste

3 tablespoons unsalted butter, divided

2 medium red bell peppers, roasted (*see page 193*) and thickly sliced

4 slices meaty bacon, fried until crisp and roughly crumbled into bite-size pieces

1. Preheat oven to 300°.

2. In a small saucepan, combine maple syrup and jalapeño over medium-high heat. Bring to a low boil, reduce heat, and simmer for 3 minutes. Remove from heat, set aside to cool slightly, and taste. Remove jalapeño if desired, or allow pepper to steep in syrup as it cools for a spicier flavor.

3. Use a 3½- to 4-inch round cookie cutter or a knife to trim brioche or hamburger buns into 4 circles. In a medium bowl, whisk together 2 eggs, milk, salt, and cayenne. Place 1 bread round in bowl, let soak up milk for 10 to 15 seconds, gently flip, and soak on other side. Transfer to a plate and repeat with remaining bread.

4. In a large oven-proof sauté pan, heat 2 tablespoons butter over medium-high heat. When foam subsides, add bread rounds and sauté until light golden brown, about 1 minute. Flip and brown on opposite side, about 30 seconds. Transfer pan to oven and bake bread until springy to touch but still moist, about 4 to 5 minutes.

5. Meanwhile, in a large nonstick sauté pan, heat remaining tablespoon butter over medium-high heat. When foam subsides, add remaining 4 eggs, cover, and cook until whites are firm but yolks are still runny, about 5 minutes. Trim whites to separate eggs, if necessary.

6. To serve, place pain perdu on 4 plates and top each with 1 sunny-side-up egg. Divide roasted peppers and bacon among plates and drizzle with spiced maple syrup. Serve immediately with additional maple syrup on the side.

HOMEMADE QUARK WITH BERRIES & HONEY

Quark, the tangy farmer's cheese popular in Central and Eastern Europe, typically has a thick, almost ricotta-like texture. It's used in everything from strudel to cheesecakes.

Homemade versions are more like Greek yogurt, so it's great for breakfast with fruit and nuts. In Bavaria, there are also some interesting savory versions spiced with chives and onions, eaten like a cheese spread on rye bread, if that's more your thing. It's so easy to make that you're going to wonder why you've been spending so much time in the yogurt aisle.

MAKES ABOUT 2 CUPS

1. Combine warm (but not hot) milk and buttermilk in medium nonreactive bowl and cover with plastic wrap. Set aside at warm room temperature until milk thickens to yogurt-like consistency, 12 to 18 hours. If milk does not thicken, discard and start again with a fresh container of buttermilk.

2. Line a fine-mesh strainer with cheesecloth or coffee filters (if cone-shaped, trim coffee filters to lay flat) and set over a deep bowl. Ladle thickened milk into strainer. Cover loosely with plastic wrap and refrigerate for 24 hours, occasionally discarding liquid whey that has accumulated in the bottom of the bowl. Transfer to a clean glass or ceramic bowl, add salt, and whisk well to incorporate. Refrigerate, covered, for up to 1 week.

3. To serve, top quark with berries and nuts and drizzle with honey.

4 cups whole milk, lukewarm

¼ cup whole or low fat cultured buttermilk

Generous pinch finely ground salt

To serve

Mixed fresh berries

Assorted toasted nuts, such as almonds, hazelnuts, and walnuts

Honey, to taste

TRI-BERRY SCONES

The word "scone" here is really more of an excuse to break the morning pie barrier. These aren't difficult to make, but with so many berries in the filling, the scones need to be partially frozen before baking.

Be sure to use a rimmed baking sheet to catch all of the fruit juices, and if using strawberries, slice them so they lie flat.

MAKES 8 SCONES

1. In a large bowl, whisk together flour, ⅓ cup sugar, baking powder, and salt. Work butter into dry ingredients with your fingers until mixture resembles a coarse meal.

2. In a small bowl, whisk together 1 egg, buttermilk, and vanilla extract, then add to flour mixture. Mix with your hands until dough just holds together like pie dough. If needed, add 1 additional tablespoon of buttermilk, but do not over-moisten dough (add no more than 2 tablespoons). Divide dough in half, and shape each half into a roughly 6 by 4-inch rectangle. Wrap in plastic wrap and refrigerate for 2 hours.

3. Cover a rimmed baking sheet that will fit in your freezer with parchment paper and dust lightly with flour. Flour a work surface and roll out one half of dough into roughly a 12 by 6-inch rectangle, flouring the top as needed. Transfer to baking sheet. Roll out second half of dough to same size.

4. Toss together frozen berries and remaining 2 tablespoons sugar, and scatter berries on top of dough on baking sheet. Place second rectangle of dough on top, pressing gently to loosely adhere. Slice dough in half lengthwise, wipe off knife blade or bench scraper with a paper towel, and slice in half widthwise. Wipe off blade again, and make two diagonal cuts from corner to corner to form 8 pie-like triangles. Slightly separate each scone so at least 1 inch of space is between each. Freeze for 1 hour, uncovered.

5. Meanwhile, preheat oven to 400°. Place baking rack in middle of oven.

6. In a small bowl, whisk together remaining egg and 3 tablespoons water, and brush scones with egg wash. Bake until scones are puffy and just beginning to lightly brown along edges, about 22 to 26 minutes, rotating sheet pan front to back halfway through. Remove from oven, and cool on baking sheet for 5 minutes. Transfer to a wire rack. Serve warm or at room temperature.

2¾ cups flour, plus more for rolling out dough

⅓ cup plus 2 tablespoons sugar, divided

2 teaspoons baking powder

½ teaspoon kosher salt

½ cup (4 ounces) unsalted butter, slightly softened but still firm

2 large eggs, divided

½ cup buttermilk, plus 1 to 2 tablespoons, if needed

1 teaspoon vanilla extract

10 ounces (about 2¼ cups) frozen mixed berries such as raspberries, blackberries, blueberries, and strawberries (strawberries sliced)

MULTIGRAIN SCONES

Like the best rustic German breads, these scones are packed with whole grains and seeds. This version is more home-pantry-friendly than the bakery version, but just as full of traditional flavor.

MAKES 8 SCONES

2 medium oranges

⅓ cup plain whole milk, yogurt, or sour cream

½ cup raisins, preferably a mix of dark and golden, packed

1¼ cups old-fashioned rolled oats

¼ cup whole flax seeds

¼ cup raw white sesame seeds

¼ cup raw shelled sunflower seeds

2 cups plus 1 tablespoon flour, plus more for dusting

1½ teaspoons baking powder

¼ teaspoon baking soda

¼ teaspoon kosher salt

½ cup plus 2 tablespoons (5 ounces total) unsalted butter, room temperature

½ cup sugar

1 large egg

1. The night before you plan to bake, finely zest both oranges. Combine zest and yogurt in a small bowl, cover, and refrigerate. Juice oranges into a small bowl, add raisins, and let stand at room temperature overnight.

2. Preheat oven to 325°. Place racks in middle of oven and line a large baking sheet with parchment paper or a silicone baking mat.

3. In a medium bowl, mix together oats, flax, sesame, and sunflower seeds. In another bowl, mix together flour, baking powder and soda, and salt.

4. In the bowl of a stand mixer fitted with the paddle attachment, combine butter, sugar, and yogurt-orange zest mixture. Mix on medium-low speed until well combined, about 1 minute. Strain raisins (discard any remaining orange juice). Add raisins and oat-seed mixture to butter. Mix well to combine, about 30 seconds. Add half of flour mixture and mix well. Add remaining flour and mix again until dough just comes together, about 30 seconds. Dough should be crumbly, like biscuit dough. Remove from stand mixer and press dough together with your hands.

5. Turn dough onto a lightly floured surface. Cut in half, then cut each half in quarters to make 8 sections. Shape each into 3-inch rounds about 1 inch thick. Place scones on baking sheet about 1½ inches apart.

6. In a small bowl, whisk together egg and 3 tablespoons water to make an egg wash. Brush egg wash over scones (discard any leftover). Bake until golden brown on bottom and light brown on top, about 35 to 38 minutes, rotating baking sheet from front to back halfway through. Allow to cool on baking sheet for 5 minutes. Transfer to a wire rack to cool completely.

RHUBARB STREUSEL KUCHEN

I think most people focus a little too much on the streusel atop their coffee cake. Don't get me wrong, the crumbly topping adds a lot of texture and flavor. But it only works in conjunction with a really moist, rich cake.

This citrusy version almost melts in your mouth, with little bits of slightly sour rhubarb that contrast with the crunchy, sweet topping. The cake also travels well, no refrigeration required, so it's become my go-to for picnic baskets for the Hollywood Bowl or the beach.

MAKES 1 9-INCH CAKE

Cake

½ cup (4 ounces) unsalted butter, melted, more for buttering pan

8 ounces rhubarb (about 2 medium stalks), ends trimmed

1¼ cups plus 1 tablespoon sugar, divided

3 large eggs

1 teaspoon lemon zest

1 teaspoon orange zest

1½ teaspoons vanilla extract

2 cups flour

1½ teaspoons baking powder

½ teaspoon kosher salt

¾ cup whole milk

Streusel

½ cup (4 ounces) unsalted butter, melted

⅔ cup sugar

½ teaspoon vanilla extract

½ teaspoon freshly squeezed lemon juice

1 large egg

1¾ cups flour

Generous pinch kosher salt

½ teaspoon baking powder

1. Preheat oven to 350° and place rack in middle of oven. Lightly grease a 9-inch square or round baking pan with butter.

2. To make the cake, slice each rhubarb stalk lengthwise in two or three pieces, as you would a thick stalk of celery, then slice widthwise into ¼-inch-thick pieces. You should have about 2 cups. In a medium bowl, toss rhubarb with 1 tablespoon sugar.

3. In a large bowl, whisk together remaining 1¼ cups sugar, eggs, lemon and orange zests, and vanilla extract until smooth.

4. In another bowl, mix together flour, baking powder, and salt. Add ⅓ of flour mixture to egg mixture and whisk until well combined. Add half of milk and mix again. Repeat with another third of flour mixture, milk, then final third of flour, whisking until just combined. A few lumps should remain. Whisk in melted butter until just incorporated. Pour cake batter into prepared pan.

5. To make the streusel, in a medium bowl, combine melted butter (it should not be hot), sugar, vanilla extract, and lemon juice. Add egg, whisk again, then add flour and salt. Sprinkle baking powder evenly over the top and fold together butter and flour mixture with a large spoon until mixture resembles a coarse meal.

6. Scatter rhubarb on top of cake batter and crumble streusel on top, breaking up any large pieces. Bake until streusel is light golden brown, cake is springy to the touch, and tester comes out clean, about 45 to 50 minutes. Place on a wire rack and cool for at least 20 minutes before serving.

BLUEBERRY VARIATION: Substitute 2 cups of blueberries for rhubarb.

Kaffee Kuchen *(Coffee Cake)*

What we call coffee cake today evolved from streusel kuchen, the yeasted crumb cakes of northern and central Europe. (*Streusel* means crumb topping.) The coffee side of the name came later, as coffee became popular in Europe. The cakes landed in America when settlers like the Pennsylvania Dutch (meaning Deutsch, or German-speakers) brought their lightly sweetened crumb cake recipes. By the late nineteenth century, the word "kaffeeklatsch" literally meant gossiping over coffee and cake. Over time, the cakes evolved into countless variations, but the simple hand-mixing technique hasn't changed, even in the electronic kitchen era.

BIRCHER MUESLI

Authentic muesli, made with raw oats, is worlds apart from the crunchy granolas found in the United States. It was developed by Swiss physician Maximilian Bircher-Benner as a health food in the early 1900s. Schliengen, the town in southern Germany where I grew up, was very close to the Swiss border. My father worked on the Swiss side in Basel as a fleischer *(butcher) in a small grocery store, where they made delicious muesli. Whenever I stopped by after school, I'd eat it by the cupful.*

Muesli by nature is very filling, so these days I prefer fresh milk and cream over the more traditional condensed milk, and a lot more fresh fruit. Toss all the ingredients together before you go to bed, and you've got an instant homemade power breakfast. It tastes even better the second and third day, so I always double or triple the recipe.

MAKES 4 SERVINGS

1. In a medium bowl, combine grated apples and lemon juice. Toss well. Add hazelnuts or almonds, raisins, honey, milk, cream, orange juice, salt, and oats, mixing thoroughly to coat oats well. Cover with plastic wrap and refrigerate overnight.

2. To serve, spoon muesli into bowls and top with berries. Refrigerate up to 5 days.

2 large unpeeled Granny Smith apples, grated

2 tablespoons freshly squeezed lemon juice

⅓ cup roughly chopped hazelnuts or almonds, toasted (*see page 193*)

¼ cup raisins

2 tablespoons honey, warmed in the microwave or on the stovetop for 5 seconds

1½ cups whole milk

1 cup heavy cream

¼ cup freshly squeezed orange juice

Generous pinch coarse sea or kosher salt

2 cups old-fashioned rolled oats

1 cup mixed berries, for serving

QUINOA BENEDICT

With these quinoa patties, the vegetables soak overnight with the oats, so you're halfway to a quick vegetarian brunch by the time you wake up. The patties freeze well, so I like to make a few extra to have around for a quick breakfast or for our Quinoa Burgers (see recipe page 73).

The only trick is shaping the patties. Like crab cakes, it takes a little subtle convincing to get them to stick together at first. But once you get the hang of it, it really is very easy.

MAKES 4 QUINOA BENEDICTS PLUS 4 ADDITIONAL QUINOA PATTIES

Quinoa Patties

½ medium zucchini, roughly chopped

6 button mushrooms, roughly chopped

1 small chayote squash, pitted, peeled, and roughly chopped

1 medium red bell pepper, seeded and roughly chopped

1 medium carrot, peeled and grated on smallest holes of box grater

½ cup old-fashioned oats

1 teaspoon coarse sea or kosher salt

2 medium cloves garlic, minced

1-inch piece ginger, peeled and finely grated

4 large eggs, divided

½ cup grated parmesan

1 cup unseasoned, toasted bread-crumbs (*recipe page 21*), divided

1 cup quinoa, cooked according to package directions and drained

½ cup flour, more if needed

¼ cup vegetable oil, divided, more if needed

Benedicts

Wilted spinach or Creamed Spinach (*recipe page 50*)

4 Crispy Poached Eggs (*recipe page 50*)

½ cup Marinara (*recipe page 105*), optional

Freshly ground pepper, to taste

1. In a food processor, combine zucchini, mushrooms, squash, and bell pepper and quickly pulse until finely chopped, about 15 to 20 times, scraping down sides of processor as needed (do not over-process vegetables into a paste). Remove any large pieces and discard them. Place processed vegetables in a strainer with grated carrots. Squeeze out as much water as possible with your hands. Place vegetables in a large bowl, add oats, and toss to combine. Cover with plastic wrap and refrigerate at least 12 hours or overnight.

2. The next day, in a large bowl, whisk together salt, garlic, ginger, 2 eggs, parmesan, and ½ cup breadcrumbs. Add vegetable-oat mixture and cooked quinoa. Mix well to combine and set aside to rest for 10 minutes. Shape mixture into 8 generous ½ cup patties, cupping each firmly together like a crab cake and flattening into rounds about 3½ inches in diameter. Freeze on a plastic wrap–lined cutting board for 20 minutes.

3. In a small bowl, whisk together remaining 2 eggs and ⅓ cup water. Place flour in another small bowl, and remaining ½ cup breadcrumbs in a third bowl.

4. Remove patties from freezer and gently dredge in flour one at a time. Sprinkle top of each patty with flour, using your hands to slightly re-shape if needed. Dip each in egg wash, then in breadcrumbs.

5. In a medium sauté pan, heat 2 tablespoons vegetable oil over medium heat. Sauté 2 to 3 patties at a time until golden brown on one side, about 3 to 4 minutes. Carefully flip with a large spatula and cook on opposite side until golden brown, another 2 to 3 minutes. Transfer to paper towels to drain. If oil begins to burn, wipe

out pan and add another 2 tablespoons oil. Repeat with remaining patties. If you want to save some patties for later, place uncooked patties on a plastic wrap–lined cutting board, place in freezer to freeze completely, then transfer to food storage bags and store in the freezer. Bring them to room temperature before frying.

6. To assemble the Quinoa Benedict, divide 4 warm quinoa patties among plates and top each with wilted or creamed spinach, a poached egg, and marinara, if desired. Season with pepper to taste and serve immediately.

MIX & MATCH BREAKFAST STAPLES

Part of the fun of cooking in L.A. is the no-holds-barred nature of it. Hot and cold mixed with spicy and sweet? Yes. Crunchy and soft combined with Asian and German flavors? Yes. Anything goes, as long as it satisfies. With the basic recipes that follow, you can mix and match to create your own modern version of a German breakfast.

CANDIED PECAN BACON

Partially cooking the bacon first renders some of the fat so the sugar doesn't absorb it all. Use good-quality, regular-cut bacon. Thin strips tend to burn before they caramelize. Crumble leftover candied bacon over salads, or use it to make just about any sandwich even better.

MAKES 5 TO 6 SERVINGS

1. Preheat oven to 375°.

2. Line bottom of 2 rimmed baking sheets with foil. Arrange bacon side by side on 1 baking sheet so pieces fit snugly together but do not overlap. (Reserve any thin-cut end slices for another use.) Bake until fat partially renders and bacon just begins to color around edges, about 15 minutes, rotating pan front to back halfway through.

3. Meanwhile, mix brown sugar, cinnamon, and nuts in a small bowl. Remove bacon from oven and transfer with tongs to reserved foil-lined baking sheet. Sprinkle bacon evenly with brown sugar mixture, pressing down lightly with a spatula to adhere.

4. Reduce oven to 325°. Return bacon to oven and bake until golden brown, about 16 to 20 minutes, rotating pan front to back halfway through. Watch bacon closely for the last 5 minutes to avoid burning. It should be golden brown but still look moist; it will continue to crisp as it cools. Transfer with tongs to a wire rack to cool for 5 minutes before serving.

1 pound regular-cut bacon, about ¼-inch thick

⅓ cup brown sugar, firmly packed

1 teaspoon cinnamon

⅓ cup roughly chopped pecans or walnuts

CRISPY POACHED EGGS WITH CREAMED SPINACH

Coat soft-boiled eggs in breadcrumbs and deep fry them, and you get a crunchy, schnitzel-like crust with the oozy yolk of a poached egg. Pretty fantastic. You can serve these eggs on just about any-thing: a classic Benedict, spinach salad, or even a simple hunk of crusty bread is hard to beat—all the better with some Black Forest ham.

The only trick is boiling the eggs so the whites are firm but the yolks stay runny. Watch the clock, and have a bowl of ice water ready. I like to boil a few extra eggs in case one breaks when peeling. Worst case, you've got one or two to "sample" in the kitchen (chef's prerogative). Use older eggs, which tend to be easier to peel than those that are super fresh.

MAKES 4 SERVINGS

Creamed Spinach

1 tablespoon unsalted butter

1 tablespoon flour

⅔ cup heavy cream

1 bunch baby spinach, tough stems removed, rinsed, and dried

Pinch freshly ground nutmeg

Coarse sea or kosher salt and freshly ground pepper, to taste

Crispy Poached Eggs

4 to 6 whole large eggs, room temperature, plus 2 large eggs, lightly beaten

⅓ cup flour

⅓ cup toasted, finely ground breadcrumbs (*recipe page 21*), plus more if needed

Vegetable oil, for frying

Freshly grated parmesan, for serving

Toasted brioche (*recipe page 26*) or other bread, for serving

1. To make spinach, in a medium saucepan, heat butter over medium-high heat. When foam subsides, whisk in flour and cook for 1 minute. Slowly add cream, whisking constantly, and cook until slightly thickened, about 30 seconds. Add spinach and stir until just wilted, about 30 seconds to 1 minute, depending on size. When cool enough to handle, purée ¼ of spinach in a blender or food processor and return to saucepan. Season with nutmeg, salt, and pepper to taste.

2. To make eggs, fill a medium bowl with ice water (use a generous amount of ice).

3. Fill a medium saucepan with about 3 inches of water and bring to a vigorous boil over high heat. Reduce heat to medium and carefully add whole eggs, one by one, with tongs or a spoon. Cook for exactly 5 minutes. Immediately remove eggs from heat and transfer to ice water. Allow to cool for 20 minutes.

4. Meanwhile, place flour, beaten eggs, and breadcrumbs in 3 separate small bowls. Line a plate with paper towels.

5. When eggs are cool, gently tap all over on the counter until shell is shattered. Lightly roll each egg between your hands and peel while submerging eggs again in ice water (water makes peeling easier). Don't vigorously break the shells or the whites will break. Roll peeled eggs lightly in flour, dip in egg wash, and roll in breadcrumbs. Make sure all sides are well coated.

6. In a small, deep saucepan, heat about 2 inches of oil to 375° degrees, or until a few breadcrumbs bubble vigorously when added. When oil is hot, fry 2 eggs at a time until golden brown, about 40 to 50 seconds; do not overcook or yolks will be firm. Carefully transfer with a slotted spoon to paper towel–lined plate and sprinkle with salt.

7. To serve, divide spinach among 4 shallow soup bowls, place an egg in center of each, and sprinkle with parmesan. Serve immediately with toasted bread.

FENNEL SAUSAGE

Yes, I'm German, and my father was a butcher. And yet my favorite sausage recipe is from an Italian butcher. My former mother-in-law used to buy incredible fennel sausages from an Italian butcher in Chicago. When he closed up the shop, she begged and begged until he finally handed over the recipe.

You can put these sausages in traditional casings, make patties for breakfast, or shape them into meatballs (see recipe page 105) to make delicious sub sandwiches. And they make an excellent Italian-style pizza topping.

———————————— MAKES ABOUT 3 POUNDS ————————————

4 pounds bone-in pork butt

3 tablespoons fennel seeds

2 teaspoons crushed red pepper flakes

1 tablespoon freshly ground pepper

1 tablespoon plus 2 teaspoons coarse sea or kosher salt

1. Trim outer edge of fat from pork butt, roughly chop fat into ½-inch pieces, and place in a medium bowl. Chop meat into equally small pieces and place in a large baking dish or in 2 smaller dishes that will fit in your freezer.

2. Continue to chop meat and fat separately, discarding tough silverskin. If any meatier pieces are tough due to a high fat ratio, place those in the fat dish. Spread out meat and fat in a single layer in separate dishes and freeze for 20 minutes.

3. If you have a meat grinder or food processor attachment, use it to grind both meat and fat according to manufacturer's instructions.

4. Remove fat from freezer. Place ½ in food processor and process until finely ground, about 20 seconds (fat will clump together). Place in a large bowl and repeat with remaining fat. Transfer to large bowl.

5. Remove meat from freezer. Place ⅓ of meat in food processor and pulse (do not process) until roughly ground, about 25 to 30 times quickly. Meat should not clump together like fat. Return to baking dish. Repeat two more times with remaining meat. Spread out in single layer and freeze for 10 minutes.

6. Meanwhile, heat a small sauté pan over medium-high heat. Add fennel seeds and toast until fragrant and just beginning to brown, about 1½ to 2 minutes, stirring often. Add to ground pork fat along with red pepper flakes, pepper, and salt.

7. Remove meat from freezer, place ⅓ in food processor, and pulse until roughly the size of small pellets, about 30 to 40 pulses. Meat will be varying sizes and should not clump together or be as finely ground as the fat. Discard any large bits of gristle. Use your hands to mix the meat into the seasoned fat mixture. Mix well.

8. Cover and refrigerate sausage overnight to allow flavors to develop. To cook, shape into 2-inch patties, flatten slightly, and fry over medium-high heat until no longer pink, about 5 to 6 minutes.

9. Refrigerate uncooked sausage for up to 5 days or freeze in small batches. To freeze as shaped patties or meatballs, shape and place in a single layer on a plastic wrap-lined cutting board. Freeze until solid, then transfer to freezer bags.

Homemade Sausages

If you have a meat grinder or a stand mixer grinder attachment, you're probably halfway to becoming an amateur meister (master) wurst-maker, a rigorous and very serious multi-year apprenticeship program in Germany.

If you don't have a meat grinder, you still need to grind your own meat. I never thought I would say this, but you actually can make good sausage in a food processor. As good as with a meat grinder? No. But still very good. The ground pork you find at grocery stores is too uniform and lacks enough fat to make good sausages. Look for pork butt with a nice, thick layer of fat. So much boneless pork butt today is over-trimmed. Bone-in cuts often have a better fat ratio (save the bone for stock). The trick is to freeze the pork first, and then grind the meat and fat separately so the meat doesn't get over-ground. But please, don't tell your local wurstmeister.

HANS'S RÖSTI POTATOES

Every time we host a dinner party, my wife, Patti, makes her salad (see recipe page 66) *and I make these Swiss-style hash browns. Yes, they're just shredded potatoes, simply dressed with salt and pan fried, but they're so much more.*

Traditionally, you steam the potatoes first, but I prefer this updated version with raw potatoes. For one, they're easier to make. You also get this really great crust, and the hash brown—like interior almost gets creamy. If you're going for a full-on flip, a nonstick skillet works best with the gently sloped sides. Otherwise, you'll get more of a deep brown color with a cast-iron skillet. Just use a plate for easier flipping.

MAKES 4 TO 5 SERVINGS

2½ pounds (about 4 medium) rus-set potatoes, scrubbed and peeled

1 teaspoon coarse sea or kosher salt, more to taste

1 tablespoon vegetable oil, more if not using a nonstick pan

4 tablespoons (2 ounces) unsalted butter, roughly chopped into ½-inch cubes

Freshly ground pepper, to taste

1. Grate potatoes on matchstick plate of a mandoline, grating plate of a food processor, or largest holes of a box grater. You should have about 4 cups, packed. Transfer to a large bowl and toss with 1 teaspoon salt.

2. Rub a 10-inch nonstick sauté pan with oil, coating sides well. Heat pan over medium-high heat and evenly scatter potatoes throughout. With a large spoon, firmly press potatoes down, especially at edges, so a slight mound forms in center like a layer cake. Cover and cook for 5 minutes. Remove lid and continue to cook, gently shaking pan occasionally, until bottom is golden brown, about 5 minutes longer. Check by gently lifting up a corner with a rubber spatula.

3. To flip rösti, remove pan from heat. If you're feeling adventurous, flip the potato in the air like a pancake. Otherwise, place a plate on top of pan. Use a kitchen towel or oven mitts to flip skillet and place rösti on the plate, then return rösti to pan with bottom side now facing up.

4. Reduce heat to medium and continue to cook potatoes, uncovered, until golden brown on bottom and potatoes are tender, about 15 minutes, shaking pan occasionally. Use a knife to test tenderness of potatoes in center. Scatter butter around edges and allow to melt into potatoes for a minute. Slide rösti onto a plate, cool for 10 minutes, and cut into wedges. Season generously with salt and pepper and serve immediately.

CALIFORNIA HASH

This version is a colorful mix of baby carrots, sunchokes, and kale, but you can use whatever produce is in season in this versatile vegetable hash. Poached eggs are always a good breakfast or light supper addition, or simply serve the vegetables on their own as a side dish.

MAKES 4 SERVINGS

1. Preheat oven to 350°.

2. If carrots are small, leave whole. If larger, slice in half or quarter. Roughly cut sunchokes into 1-inch-thick pieces. In a medium bowl, toss carrots and sunchokes with 1 tablespoon olive oil and ¼ teaspoon salt. Roast vegetables on a rimmed baking sheet until crisp-tender, 18 to 22 minutes.

3. In a large sauté pan, heat remaining 1 tablespoon olive oil and butter over medium-high heat, add red onion, and cook until just beginning to brown, 4 to 5 minutes. Add corn kernels, cook for 1 minute, then add carrots and sunchokes. Stir in kale and cook until just wilted, about 2 minutes. Season with salt and pepper to taste. Divide hash among 4 plates, top with poached egg, if desired, and drizzle with Romesco Sauce. Serve immediately.

2 pounds assorted heirloom baby or medium-size carrots, washed but not peeled

5 medium (about ½ pound) sunchokes, peeled

2 tablespoons extra-virgin olive oil, divided

½ teaspoon kosher salt, divided, more to taste

1 tablespoon unsalted butter

½ medium red onion, thinly sliced into half moons

1 fresh corn cob, kernels scraped from cob

1 small bunch kale, stalks removed and leaves roughly chopped

Freshly ground pepper to taste

Small handful of parsley leaves

4 Crispy Poached Eggs (*recipe page 50*), optional

¼ cup Romesco Sauce (*recipe page 200*), more to taste

MITTAGESSEN HOUR

AMERIKANISCH AT LUNCHTIME

After thirty years, lunch is probably where my cooking style has become the most Amerikanisch—at least in terms of influences.

As in most European countries and the United States, lunch used to be the main meal of the day. You'd go home from work or school, sit down with your family, and have a hot meal together. When I step back and look at many of the recipes I serve at my restaurants for mittagessen (lunch), I really see the influence of living in California all these years.

I arrived in the United States during a very different restaurant era. Remember those modernist, art-like squiggles of sauce off to the side? "Perfect" presentation and cultural veracity were the nose-to-tail trends of those times. We didn't mix and match flavors from different cultures like we do today. The focus was on the authenticity of regional dishes, and on making them with artistic flair.

Today, when it seems like everyone shops at farmers' markets and has an edible garden, we can take for granted having access to such an incredible range and quality of produce. But twenty-five years ago, many restaurant chefs were more obsessed with sourcing the most exotic ingredients from across the globe. Fortunately, California was well ahead of the move toward local products. We've always had an abundance of fantastic, locally grown produce, from artichokes, avocados, and asparagus to blood oranges, heirloom tomatoes, squashes, and peppers in every color. Discovering the bounty that had been sitting right in front of us was—and still is—the most exciting aspect of cooking in Kalifornien. It inspires me every day.

My lunchtime dishes have also been affected by L.A.'s cultural diversity, something I didn't grow up with in Germany. I remember the first time I ate a Chinese chicken salad. Although I later learned how American it is, at the time I thought it was so exotic, with its soy sauce, ginger, and sesame seeds. The more time I spent in L.A., the more I tasted ingredients and dishes from all continents and cultures, and the more those influences showed up in my cooking.

Over the years, we've all loosened up in the kitchen. The more we're exposed to new things, the more our cooking evolves. It's a natural progression, one that chefs and home cooks share. But for me, at least, around mittagessen hour, things haven't changed all that much. I still just want a really good lunch.

BLACKENED TOMATO SANDWICH

Finally, a spicy sandwich that takes ripe tomatoes to places their fried green colleagues have long gone. Be sure to use ripe but firm—really firm—tomatoes. If they're too juicy, they won't fry up well.

MAKES 4 SANDWICHES

1. In a small bowl, combine flour, paprika, cayenne, garlic powder, coriander, cumin, and salt and mix well. Dip tomato slices into this flour mixture, flipping to coat both sides, and set aside. Line a plate with paper towels.

2. In a medium sauté pan, heat olive oil over medium-high heat until very hot. Add 4 tomato slices and fry until just beginning to blacken, 45 to 60 seconds. Flip and fry on opposite side another 30 to 45 seconds. Set aside on paper towel–lined plate. Sprinkle tomatoes with lime zest and a pinch of salt. Repeat with remaining tomatoes, wiping out pan and adding more oil if it begins to burn.

3. To assemble sandwiches, divide 1 tablespoon aioli between each ciabatta roll or 2 slices of sourdough. Layer with avocado, 2 fried tomato slices, and lettuce. Top with remaining half of ciabatta or sourdough and slice sandwiches in half. Serve immediately.

½ cup flour

1½ tablespoons smoked paprika

½ teaspoon cayenne pepper

½ teaspoon garlic powder

½ teaspoon ground coriander

½ teaspoon ground cumin

¼ teaspoon coarse sea or kosher salt, more to taste

2 to 3 medium beefsteak tomatoes, sliced about 1 inch thick to yield 8 slices

2 tablespoons extra-virgin olive oil, more as needed

Zest of 1 lime

4 tablespoons Chipotle Aioli *(recipe page 197)*, divided

4 ciabatta rolls or 8 thin slices rustic sourdough, lightly toasted

2 large avocados, sliced

½ medium head crispy lettuce, such as iceberg or romaine

THE CALIFORNIA WALDORF

Take the basic principles of a Waldorf salad, but swap puréed celery root as the stand-in for mayonnaise and you get this subtly German hybrid of the American classic. As you work your way through the salad, the celery root and tangy lemon juice create a dressing. You can add chicken, as we do at the café, but this is a very satisfying and flavorful salad on its own.

Like artichokes, raw celery root oxidizes quickly, so have the cooking water ready when you slice them, or rub them with the side of a sliced lemon. Save the parsley-like green tops for soup stock.

MAKES 4 SIDE SALADS

1. In a medium saucepan, bring 3 cups water to a boil. Add celery root and salt, reduce to a simmer, and cook until very tender when pierced with a fork, 12 to 16 minutes. Strain over a bowl to reserve cooking water, and set celery root aside to cool slightly.

2. Meanwhile, slice unpeeled apples into thin, matchstick-like pieces by slicing each quarter thinly lengthwise, stacking slices, and slicing again lengthwise. (Alternatively, use the matchstick plate on a mandoline.) Place apples in a large bowl with celery, raisins, and pistachios. Add 3 tablespoons olive oil and 3 tablespoons lemon juice and toss well. Season with salt and additional lemon juice to taste.

3. In a blender, purée celery root with remaining 3 tablespoons olive oil and ½ cup reserved cooking water until smooth, about 10 seconds. Add more cooking water as needed, a few tablespoons at a time, to make an applesauce-like purée. Season with a pinch of salt.

4. To serve, spoon celery root purée on 4 salad plates into a 4-inch circle. Pile apple salad on top and serve immediately.

1 medium (about 8 to 10 ounces) celery root, peeled and roughly chopped into 1-inch pieces

½ teaspoon coarse sea or kosher salt, more to taste

6 medium Pink Lady apples or a similar sweet, crispy variety, quartered

6 medium stalks celery, thinly sliced

¼ cup raisins

¼ cup chopped pistachios

6 tablespoons extra-virgin olive oil, divided

3 tablespoons freshly squeezed lemon juice, more to taste

Pinch sea salt

THE CRUNCH

I used to "walk the line" a lot at 3 Square Café. Meaning, I'd grab a bowl and head down the kitchen line, picking up whatever our cooks had prepped that day: a few crunchy sliced radishes, red onions, steamed green beans. That's exactly how this salad evolved.

I like to think of this recipe as more of a blueprint, a way to make good use of unexpected finds at the market, like cucumbers or cherry tomatoes or whatever else you stumble upon. You can find romaine hearts in the produce section of most grocery stores, or use the super-crunchy little gem lettuces that are often seen at farmers' markets. The key to this salad lies in its name. Use fresh, chilled, crunchy vegetables, and serve the salad on cold plates.

———————— MAKES 4 SIDE SALADS ————————

½ medium red onion, halved lengthwise, thinly sliced in half moons

1 large or 2 small romaine hearts or the equivalent baby romaine, sliced into ½ inch pieces (about 5 cups)

½ pint cherry or grape tomatoes, halved

1 small Persian cucumber, thinly sliced

3 to 4 small radishes, thinly sliced

1 cup steamed and quartered green beans, chilled

1 tablespoon chopped chives

4 to 5 tablespoons Röckenwagner House Vinaigrette

Coarse sea or kosher salt and freshly ground pepper, to taste

1. Soak red onion slices in a small bowl of ice water for 5 minutes. Drain well.

2. In a large bowl, combine red onion, lettuce, tomatoes, cucumber, radishes, green beans, and chives and toss to combine. Drizzle 4 tablespoons dressing over salad, toss again, and taste. Add additional dressing if desired. Season with salt and pepper to taste. Serve immediately.

1 teaspoon Dijon mustard

1 tablespoon honey, warmed in the microwave for 5 seconds or on the stovetop if stiff

1 tablespoon minced shallot

2½ tablespoons sherry vinegar

2½ tablespoons unseasoned rice vinegar

⅓ cup extra-virgin olive oil

2 tablespoons vegetable oil

Freshly ground pepper, to taste

RÖCKENWAGNER HOUSE VINAIGRETTE

A quick shake-and-serve salad dressing with cross-cultural Los Angeles roots.

MAKES ABOUT ¾ CUP

1. Combine all ingredients except pepper in a medium jar with a lid, cover, and shake well. Set aside for 15 minutes to allow flavors to develop. Season with pepper to taste. Shake again before serving.

PATTI'S SALAD

Yes, on one of my restaurant menus I have both a salad inspired by my ex-mother-in-law (see recipe page 67) and one named after my wife, Patti Röckenwagner, that my current mother-in-law, Susan Taija Shin, gave me. Both display equally great California-style greenery love.

MAKES 4 SMALL SIDE SALADS

½ medium red onion, halved lengthwise, thinly sliced in half moons

1 medium head romaine or iceberg lettuce, leaves separated and torn in half if large

1 small Persian cucumber, thinly sliced

½ cup thinly sliced button mushrooms

3 tablespoons Patti's Vinaigrette, more to taste

1. Soak red onion slices in a small bowl of ice water for 5 minutes. Drain well.

2. Combine red onion, lettuce, cucumber, and mushrooms in a large bowl. Toss with 3 tablespoons Patti's Vinaigrette, taste, and add additional vinaigrette to taste. Serve immediately.

3 tablespoons vegetable oil

4½ tablespoons seasoned rice vinegar, preferably Marukan

Kosher salt, to taste

PATTI'S VINAIGRETTE

This is my wife's famously light but flavorful dressing, which we serve at dinner parties at our home. Be sure to use seasoned rice vinegar.

MAKES A SCANT ½ CUP

1. Combine vegetable oil and rice vinegar in a medium jar with a lid, cover, and shake well.

2. Set aside for 15 minutes for flavors to develop. Season with salt to taste. Shake again before serving.

THE SALLY

My former mother-in-law, Sally, was the first to show me that clever California trick: Mash an avocado into red wine vinaigrette, and you've got an instant creamy dressing.

MAKES 4 SIDE SALADS

1. In a large bowl, mash together half of avocado and 4 tablespoons dressing with a fork. The avocado will emulsify the vinaigrette. Dice remaining half of avocado and set aside.

2. Add jicama and green onions to avocado dressing and mix well to coat vegetables. Add salad greens and basil, adding more vinaigrette if necessary. Gently toss salad with your hands (tongs tend to be too rough on the delicate greens). Taste and add additional dressing if desired, or season with salt and pepper to taste. Add diced avocado and tomatoes and serve immediately.

1 large Haas avocado, peeled and sliced in half

4 to 6 tablespoons Red Wine Shallot Vinaigrette, divided

½ medium jicama, peeled and sliced into thin, 2-inch-long matchsticks

4 green onions, including tender green stems, thinly sliced

6 cups (about 5 ounces) mesclun or any mix of baby salad greens

Small handful basil leaves, roughly chopped

1 medium tomato, chopped into ½-inch pieces, or ½ pint cherry tomatoes, halved

Coarse sea or kosher salt and freshly ground pepper, to taste

RED WINE SHALLOT VINAIGRETTE

Simmering shallots in wine makes a full-flavored salad dressing base.

MAKES ABOUT 1¼ CUPS

1. In a medium saucepan, bring shallot, red wine, vinegar, and bay leaf to a boil. Reduce heat to a vigorous simmer and cook until liquid has reduced by about half, about 15 minutes. Remove from heat and set aside to cool for 15 minutes.

2. Remove bay leaf and slowly whisk in olive oil. Season dressing with salt and pepper to taste and add additional olive oil if desired. Refrigerate for up to 1 week.

½ cup finely diced shallot (about 1 large shallot)

½ cup fruity red wine, such as Beaujolais

¾ cup red wine vinegar

1 dried bay leaf

¼ cup plus 3 tablespoons extra-virgin olive oil, more to taste

Kosher salt and freshly ground pepper, to taste

SUMMER CORN & SWEET PEPPER SOUP

In German, the word "korn" means any grain. There's a bit of confusion about the etymology of the word after German settlers arrived in eastern America, whether it was used in reference to rye (whiskey) or corn, but nowadays, we all know it means the grain that grows on a cob. And once shorn of their corn, those cobs make a pretty remarkable quick stock in this light but full-flavored soup.

The fresher the corn, the better; older cobs release very little sweet milk. And note that this soup is easy to double for a crowd—you can feed a lot of people, so it's the perfect appetizer for a large dinner party.

MAKES 6 SERVINGS

3 very fresh corn cobs, husks and silk removed

1½ teaspoons coarse sea or kosher salt, more to taste

6 tablespoons (3 ounces) unsalted butter

1 medium onion, roughly chopped

1 medium yellow bell pepper, seeded and roughly chopped

2 medium cloves garlic, minced

1 bay leaf

⅛ teaspoon freshly ground nutmeg, more to taste

Freshly ground pepper to taste

½ red bell pepper, seeded and diced, for garnish

1. Trim blemishes off cobs. Hold one ear of corn upright in a medium bowl and slice downward with a small paring knife to remove kernels as close to cob as possible. Repeat with remaining corn and set aside.

2. Over a small bowl, run the back of the knife blade firmly over each cob to release any remaining milk. Set aside.

3. In a medium stockpot, combine trimmed cobs, salt, and 5 cups water. Bring to a boil, reduce heat, and simmer for 30 minutes, occasionally skimming off any foam that rises to top. Discard cobs.

4. Meanwhile, in a large Dutch oven or soup pot, heat butter over medium-high heat. Sauté onion, yellow pepper, and garlic in butter until vegetables are soft, stirring occasionally, 8 to 10 minutes. Add bay leaf and all but ½ cup corn and cook for 5 minutes. Add corn milk, 2 cups corn stock, and nutmeg. Simmer until corn is tender, about 20 minutes. Remove bay leaves and set aside to cool for 30 minutes.

5. In a blender, purée soup in batches until smooth. Return to pot and stir in remaining corn stock, 1 cup at a time, until desired thickness is reached. Add remaining ½ cup corn and season with salt and pepper to taste. Divide soup among 6 bowls and garnish with diced red bell pepper. Serve immediately.

POTATO PARSNIP SOUP WITH MARJORAM

This soup gets a creamy base from puréed vegetables, a subtle sweetness from parsnips, and zip from a splash of vinegar. Use a vegetable stock and you've got dinner for everyone at the table: kids, hearty eaters, and vegans alike. World dinner table peace?

You can make this soup as smooth or chunky as you like, and if you can't find fresh marjoram, substitute half the amount of fresh oregano.

MAKES 6 SERVINGS

1. In a large Dutch oven or heavy-bottomed soup pot, heat olive oil over medium heat. Add onion, carrot, and celery and sauté, stirring occasionally, until vegetables begin to brown, 8 to 10 minutes. Add garlic, coriander, and caraway seeds and sauté for 30 seconds. Add potatoes and parsnip and continue to cook vegetables for 5 minutes, stirring occasionally. Add vinegar to deglaze, scraping up any brown bits from bottom of pan, and cook for 2 minutes. Add salt and stock, bring to a simmer, and cook until vegetables are very tender, about 15 minutes. Remove from heat.

2. Transfer 2 cups soup, including vegetables, to a blender. When cool enough to safely purée, blend until smooth. (If you don't have a professional-strength blender, do not blend when hot or steam can blow off lid.) Return to soup pot. For a creamier consistency, purée additional soup, or leave it as is for more texture. Stir in marjoram, taste, and season with additional salt and pepper as desired. Serve immediately.

2 tablespoons extra-virgin olive oil

½ large onion, roughly chopped

1 medium carrot, peeled and roughly chopped

2 medium stalks celery, roughly chopped

1 medium clove garlic, minced

¼ teaspoon ground coriander

¼ teaspoon caraway seeds, lightly crushed in a mortar and pestle

1½ pounds russet potatoes (about 4 medium), scrubbed, peeled, and diced into 1-inch pieces

1 medium parsnip, peeled, cored, and roughly chopped

1 tablespoon white wine vinegar

1 teaspoon coarse sea or kosher salt, more to taste

5 cups homemade vegetable or Brown Chicken Stock (*recipe page 195*), or low-sodium store-bought stock

2 tablespoons loosely packed fresh marjoram leaves, chopped

Freshly ground pepper, to taste

DAS SANDWICH

In the past, the German take on a sandwich was called *ein belegtes brot*—literally, a "covered/draped bread." These open-face sandwiches traditionally had a generous amount of spread—butter, schmaltz, or quark (fresh farmers' cheese)—topped with cold cuts and/or cheese. Globalization has changed all that, and in Germany today you'll find American-style sandwiches, Italian panini, and Middle Eastern wraps. What hasn't changed is the German penchant for eating these conventionally hand-held foods with a fork and knife, as if they were steaks.

QUINOA BURGER

Sure, quinoa is trendy—but for a reason. It's versatile, filling, high in protein, and gluten free. When you pack it into a patty, pan-fry it, and top it with this mix of vegetables, you'll see why the Quinoa Burger is the perennial vegetarian favorite at 3 Square Café in Venice.

MAKES 4 BURGERS

1. In a large skillet, heat ½ tablespoon olive oil over medium-high heat. Sauté bottom half of buns, cut-side down, until just beginning to brown, about 2 minutes. Set aside and repeat with remaining ½ tablespoon oil and tops of buns. Set aside.

2. Add butter to skillet. When foam subsides, add bell pepper and sauté until crisp-tender, 3 to 4 minutes. Add spinach and toss just until wilted, about 10 seconds. Remove from heat.

3. If using cheese, preheat broiler to low. To assemble burger, spread 1 tablespoon romesco sauce on each bun. Top with warm quinoa patty and ¼ of spinach–bell pepper mixture. For cheeseburgers, place 1 slice cheese on each top bun and broil until melted, about 15 seconds. Serve immediately.

1 tablespoon extra-virgin olive oil, divided

4 good-quality Brioche or Pretzel Hamburger Buns (*recipes page 20 and 26*)

1 tablespoon unsalted butter

1 red or yellow bell pepper, stemmed, seeded, and thinly sliced

2 cups baby spinach, packed

4 Quinoa Patties, fried and kept warm (*recipe page 46*)

4 tablespoon Romesco Sauce (*recipe page 200*), divided

4 thin slices good-quality cheddar, optional

Hamburger

I'm not going to pretend that quinoa has any historic connection to German food, or start another debate over whether the hamburger patty really originated in Hamburg. How can you put a definite time frame on something as fundamental as roughly chopping up meat into a patty? Hungry people have probably been doing it for a lot longer than we give them credit.

But in Germany, there is a meatloaf-like burger called a *frikadellen*, or *bouletten*, depending on what region you are in, that has been around a good while. It's basically ground raw meat. You soak a bread roll in milk, season the whole mixture with mustard and sautéed onions spiked with plenty of parsley, and form them into patties. Mini meatloaf patties, in essence. If you coat them in breadcrumbs and pan-fry them, I'm guessing you'll have a whole new burger "invention" that will impress your friends.

CALIFORNIA CLUB

This is my version of the club sandwich, West Coast style, with tomato jam and basil mayo.

MAKES 4 SANDWICHES

½ cup grated parmesan

8 thin slices sourdough bread, about 4 to 5 inches long

2 tablespoons unsalted butter, room temperature

2 to 3 tablespoons Basil Mayonnaise *(recipe page 196)*

4 pieces leftover Jidori Brick Chicken *(recipe page 120)* or Chicken Schnitzel *(recipe page 113)*, warmed

4 tablespoons Spiced Tomato Jam *(recipe page 198)*, divided

8 slices bacon, fried until crispy

1 avocado, quartered

¼ head iceberg lettuce, torn into pieces

1. Preheat oven to 350°.

2. To make parmesan crisps, line a baking sheet with parchment paper or a Silpat mat. Divide grated parmesan into 4 mounds (2 tablespoons each) several inches apart on baking sheet and gently spread into 4-inch ovals. Bake until cheese is melted, 6 to 8 minutes. Cool crisps completely on baking sheet.

3. To assemble sandwiches, butter all slices of bread on one side. Toast in pan or on a griddle until light brown and divide basil mayo among bread. Place 1 piece chicken on each bottom slice and top with 1 tablespoon tomato jam and 2 slices bacon. Thinly slice each avocado quarter and fan out on top. Finish each sandwich with a parmesan crisp and lettuce. Serve immediately.

SHRIMP GRILLED CHEESE

If you're making only two sandwiches, make the entire filling anyway. Leftovers will morph beautifully into a hot shrimp gratin appetizer.

MAKES 4 SANDWICHES

1. Preheat oven to 375°.

2. In a large sauté pan, heat olive oil over medium-high heat. Add shrimp and sauté until opaque on one side, about 1 minute. Flip and continue to cook until shrimp curl but are still translucent in center, about 1 minute. Transfer shrimp and accumulated juices to a small bowl. When cool enough to handle, roughly chop into ½-inch pieces.

3. In a medium bowl, combine cream cheese, fontina, and a pinch each of cayenne and salt. Mash with the back of a spoon or your hands until grated cheese is well incorporated. Add shrimp and pan juices and mix well. Divide shrimp-cheese mixture among 4 slices of brioche. Top each with another slice of bread and press down firmly.

4. In a clean, large sauté pan, heat 1 generous tablespoon butter over medium-high heat. When foam subsides, add 2 sandwiches and cook until golden brown on one side, about 2 minutes. Flip with a spatula, moving sandwiches around in pan to soak up butter, and continue to cook until lightly toasted on opposite side, about 1½ minutes longer. Place sandwiches on ungreased baking sheet. Repeat with remaining tablespoon of butter and sandwiches. Bake sandwiches until cheese in center is melted, 5 to 7 minutes. Cut in half and serve immediately.

1 tablespoon extra-virgin olive oil

1 pound shrimp, peeled, deveined, and tails removed

6 ounces (¾ cup) cream cheese, room temperature

2 cups grated fontina cheese, packed

Generous pinch cayenne pepper

Coarse sea or kosher salt to taste

2½ tablespoons unsalted butter, divided

8 slices brioche (*recipe page 26*) or good-quality white sandwich bread

Shrimp Gratin

If you make only two sandwiches, use the leftover shrimp mixture for this appetizer:
Preheat oven to 350°. In a small bowl, combine 3 tablespoons heavy cream and ½ of shrimp mixture. Mix well and spread into a buttered 5- or 6-inch gratin dish. Top with about 2 tablespoons grated fontina. Bake until hot and bubbly, 12 to 14 minutes. Sprinkle gratin with chopped parsley and serve immediately with crackers or Melba toast.

CITRUS-SPICED RED CABBAGE

During the holidays, slow-simmered cabbage is the traditional side served with roast goose (see recipe page 146) or duck, but it's just too good to eat only once a year. Every cook in Germany has his or her own recipe, but the basic formula is the same: red cabbage and apples, slow-braised in red wine and spices. I like to add plenty of citrus to brighten the flavors—a California thing, I guess.

Adding sugar to the onions while you cook them is the quickest route to a caramelized flavor. The only trick is finding a large enough container, and room in the fridge to brine the cabbage overnight. But the flavors really intensify after a few days, so you'll be rewarded with lunch leftovers all week. It's also really great on a leftover turkey sandwich.

MAKES 10 TO 12 SERVINGS

1 large head red cabbage, tough outer leaves removed, cored and quartered

2 medium Pink Lady apples or similar sweet, crispy variety, grated (*see page 193*)

1 tablespoon kosher salt, more to taste

1 medium orange

8 cloves

1 bottle fruity red wine, such as Beaujolais

1 cup freshly squeezed orange juice

3 juniper berries

1 cinnamon stick

2 bay leaves

3 tablespoons goose fat or extra-virgin olive oil

½ large onion, finely chopped

4 tablespoons sugar

1. Slice cabbage as thinly as possible crosswise and place in a large bowl. You should have about 10 to 12 cups. Add grated apples, sprinkle with salt, and toss to combine.

2. Spike orange all over with cloves. Slice orange into quarters without cutting through cloves.

3. Combine wine, orange juice, juniper berries, cinnamon stick, and bay leaves in a large (4-quart) plastic container or nonreactive stockpot. Add orange quarters, squeezing out most of the juice as you place them in the brine, and half of cabbage mixture. Top with remaining cabbage; it will not be completely submerged. Close container securely and refrigerate overnight or up to 24 hours. Shake container once or twice during the brining process.

4. The following day, melt goose fat or olive oil in a large, heavy-bottomed stock or soup pot over medium-high heat. Add onions and sauté until just beginning to brown, 3 to 4 minutes. Add sugar and continue to cook, stirring often, until onions are caramelized, 8 to 10 minutes.

5. Use a strainer, or just hold one hand over brined cabbage as you pour, to extract 1 generous cup liquid from the brine mix. Pour it into the pot with the onions to deglaze. Stir well, then pour remaining brine and cabbage into pot, including oranges and spices. Bring to a boil, reduce heat, and simmer until cabbage is very tender and braising liquid has reduced to about the height of the cabbage, about 2 hours, stirring occasionally. Season with salt to taste.

6. Serve immediately, or cool completely and refrigerate for up to 1 week. Reheat before serving.

PORT WINE LENTILS

With light, tangy lentil salads everywhere these days, we tend to forget that these meaty legumes also taste great with bold, full-flavored ingredients like Port. This version doubles as a picnic-packable lunch or dinner side, so I like to make a big pot.

Use good-quality lentils or they will fall apart. The cooking time and amount of liquid varies depending on the type of lentils you use, so you'll need to check up on them occasionally as they cook— a handy excuse to keep tasting the Port.

MAKES 8 TO 10 SERVINGS

1. In a medium saucepan, heat butter over medium-high heat. When foam subsides, add shallot, carrots, celery root, parsnip, and ham or bacon. Sauté until vegetables and meat begin to brown, 8 to 10 minutes. Add lentils and stir for 1 minute, then stir in tomato paste, salt, pepper, and cayenne.

2. Add Port and veal or chicken stock and bring to a simmer. Reduce heat to low, cover, and cook until lentils are tender but still firm (they will continue to cook as they cool), 22 to 30 minutes, depending on size and type of lentils. If lentils begin to look dry, add another few tablespoons of stock. Stir in balsamic vinegar and season with salt and pepper to taste. Serve warm or at room temperature.

2 tablespoons unsalted butter

½ medium shallot, finely chopped

1 medium carrot, finely chopped

¼ medium celery root, peeled and finely chopped, or 1 small stalk celery, chopped

¼ medium parsnip, peeled, cored, and finely chopped

2 thin slices Black Forest ham or prosciutto, or 1 meaty slice bacon, diced

16 ounces (about 2 cups) good-quality green lentils, such as du Puy, rinsed

1 tablespoon tomato paste

½ teaspoon coarse sea or kosher salt, more to taste

½ teaspoon freshly ground pepper, more to taste

Generous pinch cayenne pepper, more to taste

1¼ cups Port

1½ cups Brown Veal Stock *(recipe page 194)* or Brown Chicken Stock *(recipe page 195)*, more as needed

1 tablespoon balsamic vinegar, more to taste

GERMAN POTATO SALAD

Over the years, I've come to accept that what my stateside friends consider potato salad will never be what I consider potato salad. Making authentic, German-style potato salad is simple, as long as you follow each step in succession.

First, boil three or so pounds of whole potatoes—unpeeled. Use smaller potatoes or you'll be boiling all day long. While they're still warm, and here's the key, peel the potatoes and toss them in a simple dressing that includes a generous amount of ham stock (see recipe page 194). Have patience. The potatoes will gradually soak up the stock to make a creamy sauce. And please, no mayonnaise! Danke.

———— MAKES 6 TO 8 SERVINGS ————

3 pounds (about 7 to 8) small rus-set potatoes, 3 to 4 inches long, scrubbed

2½ teaspoons coarse sea or kosher salt, divided, more to taste

¼ cup vegetable oil

½ large onion, diced

2 meaty slices bacon, diced

2 teaspoons whole caraway seeds

1 teaspoon freshly ground pepper, more to taste

2 tablespoons Dijon mustard

¼ cup white wine vinegar

1¾ to 2¼ cups Ham Stock (*recipe page 194*), warm

1. In a large Dutch oven or soup pot, bring potatoes, 2 teaspoons salt, and enough cold water to cover potatoes by 2 inches to a low boil. Continue to gently boil until potatoes are just tender in center when pierced with a fork, about 20 to 25 minutes, depending on size. Strain and leave potatoes in colander to partially cool. Return pot to stove.

2. Meanwhile, in a large sauté pan, heat oil over medium-high heat. Add onion and bacon and sauté until both begin to brown around the edges, 12 to 15 minutes, stirring occasionally (bacon will still be soft). Add caraway seeds, remaining ½ teaspoon salt, pepper, and mustard and stir to combine. Transfer onion mari-nade to Dutch oven and add vinegar and 1¾ cups ham stock. Bring to a simmer and remove from heat.

3. Peel potatoes while still warm and roughly chop into ½-inch pieces. Add warm potatoes to Dutch oven with vinegar-ham stock, cover, and set aside to marinate for 20 minutes, stirring every 5 minutes. If potatoes soak up all the marinade, add remain-ing ½ cup stock. Season with salt and pepper to taste. Serve imme-diately or refrigerate for up to 3 days. Bring to room temperature before serving.

APPLE WALNUT STRUDEL

Growing up, I loved going to my aunt's house in Bavaria. She lived at the Tegernsee, truly the most picturesque lake surrounded by mountains. She would serve the lightest lunch possible, usually some kind of soup, basically as an excuse to move right on to her amazing homemade strudel. It was one of my favorite meals.

Strudel suffers from the misconception that it's difficult to make, but it's actually a very forgiving dough. And while Americans think of strudel as heavy, the classic version, with a high fruit-to-dough ratio, is actually quite light. Stretch it with your hands like pizza dough, and then wrap the paper-thin dough around the fruit filling. With so many heirloom apple varieties today, it's hard to go wrong.

SERVES 8 HUNGRY KIDS, BIG OR SMALL

1. In a large bowl, stir together flour and salt. Drizzle olive oil over top and loosely mix together with a fork. Slowly add water, ¼ cup at a time, while mixing with fork. When all water is incorporated, dough should come together and be very shaggy. Add another splash of water if dough won't come together.

2. Turn out dough onto a very lightly floured surface and knead by hand until no longer shaggy and dough forms a ball, 3 to 4 minutes. (It will not be perfectly smooth like yeasted bread.) Or, knead dough in a stand mixer fitted with the paddle attachment for about 2 minutes. Place vegetable oil in a medium bowl, dip hands in oil, and transfer dough to bowl. Roll dough in oil to completely coat, wrap in plastic, and set aside to rest at warm room temperature for 2 to 3 hours.

3. In a small sauté pan, melt 2 tablespoons butter over medium-high heat. When foam subsides, add breadcrumbs and toast, stirring occasionally, until golden brown, about 3 to 4 minutes. Set aside.

4. In a large bowl, combine apples, ⅓ cup sugar, and 2 teaspoons cinnamon. Squeeze lemon over mixture, mix well, and stir in walnuts. In a small saucepan or microwave-safe dish, melt remaining ½ cup (4 ounces) butter and set aside.

2 cups flour

¼ teaspoon kosher salt

3 tablespoons extra-virgin olive oil

¾ cup lukewarm water

2 tablespoons vegetable oil

½ cup plus 2 tablespoons (5 ounces) unsalted butter, divided

⅓ cup unseasoned breadcrumbs (*recipe page 21*)

2½ pounds (about 6 large) tangy-sweet apples like Golden Delicious, peeled, quartered, and sliced ¼-inch thick

⅓ cup plus 1 tablespoon sugar, divided

2½ teaspoons cinnamon, divided

¼ lemon

½ cup walnuts, toasted (*see page 193*) and roughly chopped into large pieces

To serve

Powdered sugar

Vanilla ice cream, optional

(continued)

5. Preheat oven to 350° and place rack in middle of oven. In a small bowl or ramekin, mix together remaining 1 tablespoon sugar and ½ teaspoon cinnamon.

6. To assemble strudel, lightly oil a work surface and place a 2-foot-long, 14-inch-wide piece of parchment paper on top. Lightly flour parchment and place dough in the center. Roll out dough lightly with a rolling pin into a rough rectangle. With your hands, continue to stretch out dough like pizza, pulling gently on all sides and in the middle until dough is about the size of the parchment paper. If dough tears in a few places, that's fine, just patch it up.

7. Brush dough generously all over with melted butter and sprinkle with toasted breadcrumbs. Trim off any thick edges around dough. Place apple-walnut mixture about 2 inches from top of dough, so you have a 3-inch-wide strip of apples running end to end horizontally. Lift the parchment paper at the top to help roll up top edge of dough halfway over the apples like a burrito. Use your fingers to gently pull and stretch dough toward you so it covers the apples. Brush newly exposed areas of dough (now the top and sides of the "burrito") with butter, then roll the mixture toward you, lightly stretching dough as you go, continuing to butter dough until you have rolled up the entire strudel.

8. Trim away all but 4 to 5 inches of parchment paper around edges and use paper to help transfer strudel to a rimmed baking pan, forming a U-shape with the strudel so it fits on the pan if necessary. Brush strudel generously with butter and sprinkle with cinnamon-sugar mixture. Bake until golden brown, 40 to 45 minutes, rotating pan front to back halfway through.

9. Allow strudel to cool for 20 minutes and sprinkle with powdered sugar. Slice into 8 pieces and serve immediately with ice cream, if desired.

STAMMTISCH

STAMMTISCH WITH THE REGULARS

In Germany, *stammtisch* are casual get-togethers held at cafés, coffee shops, or bars—the word loosely translates to "group of regulars." Small countryside restaurants will often have a stammtisch sign on a table, meaning that table has been set aside for locals, who gather to share a meal and catch up on community gossip.

I hosted my first stateside stammtisch back in the 1990s. It was a rough time to be in L.A. We had the riots, huge fires, and a big earthquake, one right after another. Everyone was a little down in the dumps. I decided to host a community event that would bring people together to break bread, have a beer or a glass of wine, and share a few small bites together. I needed it. We all needed it.

The gatherings were held at my flagship restaurant in Santa Monica on Tuesdays in the early evenings, or whenever anyone could drop by. Informality was the entire point. The traffic didn't matter, and there were no apologetic phone calls to make. You could never be late. I'd throw a few dishes, like schnitzel, homemade sausages, or spätzle together, and serve them mostly family style. We'd just eat and talk. I can't tell you how many friendships were born out of those first stammtisch. As a matter of fact, I met my wife, Patti, at one of them years ago.

I still host stammtisch as often as I can, rotating the location among my restaurants. Chefs always have been, and still are, notoriously bad about sitting down and actually enjoying a meal. We have a hard time stopping, even for just a moment. But we're not the only ones who have trouble slowing down—most everyone I know could benefit from stepping away from their computers and phones to enjoy a little relaxed time off with friends, old and new, around the stammtisch table.

GREEN HUMMUS

It's a good thing when the leftovers of a cocktail-party dip are equally delicious on the next day's sandwich.

MAKES ABOUT 2½ CUPS

1. Drain chickpeas and reserve liquid. In a food processor, combine 1 cup chickpeas (reserve remaining chickpeas for another use), ½ cup chickpea liquid, tahini, garlic, cumin, cayenne, and salt. Process until well combined, about 30 seconds, scraping down sides of processor as needed.

2. Add edamame and blend again until smooth. With processor running, pour in olive oil and lemon juice. If mixture is too thick, add additional chickpea liquid, 1 tablespoon at a time, until hummus reaches desired consistency. Add additional lemon juice and salt to taste.

3. To serve, spoon hummus into a wide, shallow serving dish. Drizzle generously with olive oil and sprinkle with parsley. Serve with sliced vegetables. You can make this in advance and store in the refrigerator for up to 5 days.

1 (15-ounce) can chickpeas

¼ cup tahini paste

2 medium cloves garlic, roughly chopped

1 teaspoon ground cumin

Generous pinch cayenne pepper, more to taste

1 teaspoon coarse sea or kosher salt, more to taste

1 (12-ounce) package (about 2 cups) frozen edamame, cooked according to package instructions and drained

3 tablespoons extra-virgin olive oil, more for serving

2 tablespoons freshly squeezed lemon juice, more to taste

2 tablespoons minced parsley

Assorted vegetables for dipping, such as sliced sweet peppers, baby radishes, carrots, and endive spears

AVOCADO CROSTINI WITH BABY RADISHES

The more milestone birthdays you celebrate in the kitchen (I've had a few), the more you appreciate when less really is more. For these crostini, look for flavorful baby radishes, like the French Breakfast variety, at the farmers' market. And now is definitely the time to pull out that really good bottle of olive oil and that quality sea salt.

MAKES 8 CROSTINI

1. Brush bread slices with 1 tablespoon olive oil. Lightly toast bread on both sides in a stovetop grill pan, on the grill, or under the broiler.

2. In a medium bowl, combine avocados, remaining 2 tablespoons olive oil, garlic, lemon juice, and a generous punch of salt. Smash avocados with a fork to make a rough paste. Add additional lemon juice and salt to taste.

3. Generously spread avocado mixture on bread slices, sprinkle with sea salt, and arrange sliced radishes on top. Drizzle with olive oil and serve immediately.

4 slices rustic sourdough bread, cut in half, or 8 smaller baguette slices

3 tablespoons extra-virgin olive oil, divided, more for drizzling

2 ripe medium avocados, peeled and sliced in half

1 small clove garlic, minced

Juice of ½ lemon, more to taste

Sel gris or other good-quality coarse sea salt, to taste

3 to 4 baby radishes, shaved on a mandoline or very thinly sliced

BACON ROSEMARY GUGELHUPF

You know all of those oversize cake pans shaped like giant castles and gingerbread houses you see in fancy kitchen boutiques? They're gugelhupf pans in disguise. The smaller American bundt cake pan was derived from the German dried-fruit-and-nut version in the 1950s by Henry Dalquist, the founder of Nordic Ware. In parts of Germany and Austria, these cakes are known as bundkuchen.

Unlike bundt cake, gugelhupf is leavened with yeast, which gives the very moist, egg-rich dough more of a bread-like texture. I let mine hupf (hop) three times, like a rabbit, and add a little baking powder for extra height. Try this savory version with a late-afternoon glass of wine. Without the herbs and bacon, it's also pretty great as a buttery dinner bread. Leftovers are a must for toast.

Note that this dough requires a lot of time to rest and rise, so it's best to make it one day in advance—which makes it ideal for entertaining.

MAKES 10 TO 12 SERVINGS

1 cup whole milk, lukewarm

2¼ teaspoons (1 package) active dry yeast

1 cup (8 ounces) unsalted butter, at room temperature, plus more for buttering pan

2 tablespoons sugar

5 cups flour, divided

1 teaspoon baking powder

1¼ teaspoons kosher salt

6 large eggs, lightly beaten, divided

5 slices meaty bacon, fried until crispy and crumbled

2 teaspoons finely chopped fresh rosemary

Crème fraîche with chives for garnish, optional

1. Combine warm (but not hot) milk and yeast in a small dish. Set aside for 5 minutes until yeast begins to bubble.

2. In a stand mixer fitted with the paddle attachment, combine butter, sugar, 2½ cups flour, baking powder, and salt. Cover stand mixer with a kitchen towel and mix on low speed for 30 seconds. Add remaining 2½ cups flour, cover, and continue to mix until flour is flecked with butter like pie crust, about 30 more seconds. Add yeast-milk mixture and mix again, scraping down paddle if needed. Add 3 eggs, mix until incorporated, and add remaining 3 eggs. Mix well, scraping down paddle and sides of bowl. Dough will be very sticky. Cover with a kitchen towel and set aside to rest in a warm spot for 20 minutes.

3. Butter your hands generously, add bacon and rosemary to dough, and mix well to incorporate. (If not using bacon and rosemary, fold dough up on itself 2 or 3 times with buttered hands or a rubber spatula.) Transfer dough to a large, lightly buttered bowl, cover with a kitchen towel, and set aside to rise in a warm spot for 1 hour. (Note: It will not double.)

4. Generously butter a large 9- or 10-inch gugelhupf or bundt pan with butter. With lightly floured hands, punch down dough, remove from bowl, and gently stretch around bottom of gugelhupf pan. Loosely pinch edges together. Cover tightly with plastic wrap, refrigerate, and let rise for 12 hours or overnight. Dough should rise more than halfway up sides of pan.

5. Preheat oven to 350° and place rack in middle of oven. Place cold gugelhupf in oven and bake until top is light golden brown and cake tester comes out clean, about 40 to 45 minutes (a smaller pan may take a few minutes longer), rotating pan front to back halfway through. Cool 10 minutes on a wire rack, then invert onto rack to cool completely. Serve with crème fraîche livened up with some chopped chives, if desired.

PRETZEL KNÖDEL

Knödel are dumplings made from day-old bread. I've been making these with pretzels for twenty years. If you don't have pretzels, you can substitute brioche.

Knödel freeze well, so I like to make enough to pull out as a last-minute appetizer or quick dinner side. To make a retro cocktail-worthy version, cut them into small pieces and spear them on toothpicks with fried ham.

MAKES ABOUT 40 COCKTAIL BITES OR 10 TO 12 SIDE-DISH SERVINGS

1 pound day-old soft pretzels or pretzel rolls (about 4; *recipe page 16*), roughly chopped or torn into 1-inch pieces

1½ cups whole milk, warmed

2 tablespoons (1 ounce) unsalted butter, divided

½ large onion, finely chopped

2 teaspoons fresh thyme leaves

½ teaspoon coarse sea or kosher salt (omit if pretzels are salted)

1 teaspoon finely ground pepper, more to taste

3 large eggs, lightly beaten

To serve

2 tablespoons (1 ounce) unsalted butter, divided

Honey Mustard and Spicy Horseradish Mustard (*recipe page 196*)

1-inch pieces ham, pan-fried, optional

1. Place pretzel pieces in a large bowl, add warm milk, and stir to combine.

2. In a medium skillet, heat 2 tablespoons butter over medium heat. Add onions and thyme, and sauté until onions are softened, about 3 to 4 minutes. Add salt and pepper and transfer to pretzel mixture. Add eggs, mix well with a rubber spatula or your hands, and set aside for 10 minutes for bread to soak up liquid.

3. Turn half of dough into center of a 16-inch piece of plastic wrap. Roughly form dough into a 10- to 12-inch log. Wrap bottom and top edges of plastic over center of dough to loosely encase. Pack dough into a compact sausage shape by twisting both ends of plastic wrap and continuing to snugly pull up the center. Tie off one end of plastic and tightly pack dough into an 8-inch sausage shape. Tie off opposite end. Dough should be very compact. Repeat with second half of dough.

4. Wrap both pieces of plastic wrap covered dough securely in foil. Fill a Dutch oven or soup pot large enough to fit both lengthwise ⅓ full of water. Bring to a boil, reduce to a simmer, and add both knödel, seam-side up. Partially cover with lid and simmer for 30 minutes; knödel should be pretty firm when pressed. Remove with tongs, drain any water that has accumulated in foil, and set aside to cool completely, about 2 hours. Remove knödel from foil and refrigerate overnight, or freeze in food storage bags.

5. To serve, if frozen, thaw completely at room temperature before cooking. Remove plastic wrap. Slice off ends and discard, and slice each knödel into about 10 ½-inch slices with a serrated knife. If making cocktail-sized pieces, quarter each log lengthwise before you slice it.

6. In a large skillet, heat 1 tablespoon butter over medium-high heat. Add 5 knödel slices, full or quartered, and sauté until dark golden brown, about 2 minutes. Flip and cook until golden brown on opposite side, about 1½ minutes. Transfer to a plate. Repeat with remaining 1 tablespoon butter and knödel. Season with salt and pepper to taste. If making cocktail-size pieces, spear 2 mini knödel on a toothpick with fried ham, if desired. Serve immediately with mustards.

HERB VARIATION: Add a generous handful of finely chopped parsley leaves to the dough.

AVOCADO FRIES WITH FIRE-ROASTED SALSA

Avocado fries are one of those ambidextrous snacks, equally at home when dressed up on a party platter with Fire-Roasted Salsa (see recipe page 199) and Herb Mayonnaise (see recipe page 196), or happy to hang out as a quick weeknight side with a squeeze of lemon juice.

The only trick is the ripeness of the avocados. Frying will not improve their flavor, so they shouldn't be too firm, but they need to be firm enough to hold together. In other words, look for ripe, but not over-ripe, avocados. I always keep an extra one or two around in case. Worst case, you'll have a few extra fries. A good thing, as they disappear quickly.

———— MAKES 24 LARGE FRIES, ABOUT 6 SERVINGS ————

1. If not serving avocado fries immediately, preheat oven to 200°. Line a baking sheet with paper towels.

2. Place flour in a wide, shallow bowl and panko in another wide, shallow bowl. In a small bowl, whisk together eggs and water.

3. In a deep, medium saucepan, heat 1½ inches of oil to 375° degrees, or until a few panko bits bubble vigorously when added.

4. Meanwhile, halve avocados lengthwise, remove pit, and slice each half into 4 pieces. Peel away skin, and coat each slice, one by one, in flour, shaking off excess. Dip in egg wash, then panko, gently pressing breadcrumbs on sides to coat. Place avocados on large cutting board or plate.

5. When oil is hot, fry 3 to 4 avocado slices at a time until golden brown, about 30 seconds. Gently transfer with tongs to paper towel–lined baking sheet and sprinkle generously with salt.

6. Place baking sheet in oven to keep warm, or serve immediately with lemon slices and salsa or other condiments (*see above*), if desired. Repeat with remaining avocado slices.

1¼ cups flour, more as needed

1½ cups panko breadcrumbs, more as needed

2 large eggs

2 tablespoons water

Vegetable oil, for frying

3 to 4 ripe, but not soft, medium Haas avocados

Coarse sea or kosher salt, to taste

To serve

Lemon wedges

Fire-Roasted Salsa (*recipe page 199*) or your favorite salsa

Herb Mayonnaise (*recipe page 196*), optional

Spiced Tomato Jam (*recipe page 198*), optional

HERBED GRAVLAX

I love gravlax, the lightly cured fish with Scandinavian roots, and have been making it since well before I opened my first restaurant in California. Traditionally, the fish is cold-cured with dill and spices, often with a splash of Aquavit, but I prefer to pile on the herbs and vegetables and finish the cure with lime juice for a brighter flavor.

Salmon is the classic curing choice. Lately, I've also been making gravlax with steelhead trout, an ocean-migrating variety from the Pacific that is sustainably farmed and widely available (sometimes called "salmon trout"). It has a mild, subtly sweet salmon-like flavor that works really well with this vegetable-friendly cure.

MAKES ABOUT 1½ POUNDS

½ small onion, roughly chopped

1 medium leek, white part only, sliced

1 medium carrot, peeled and roughly chopped

½ cup roughly chopped dill, leaves and tender top stems only

½ cup roughly chopped packed flat-leaf parsley, leaves only

¼ cup roughly chopped chives

1½ teaspoons mustard powder

½ teaspoon ground coriander

½ teaspoon crushed red pepper flakes

½ teaspoon chile powder

1 tablespoon sea salt

2 teaspoons sugar

2 tablespoons lime juice (about 1 medium lime)

1½ pounds skin-on steelhead trout or salmon (a single piece), deboned

To serve

2 or 3 sprigs dill, finely chopped

Toast, crackers, or rye bread

1. Combine onion, leek, carrot, dill, parsley, and chives in a food processor. Process until vegetables are finely chopped and form a rough paste, about 30 seconds. Transfer to a medium bowl and add mustard powder, coriander, red pepper flakes, chile powder, salt, sugar, and lime juice. Mix well.

2. Line a 9" x 13" glass pan lengthwise with a sheet of plastic wrap large enough to hang over both ends by about 6 inches. Lay another sheet of plastic wrap width-wise in pan with about a 4-inch overhang. With your hands, spread half of paste mixture on plastic wrap roughly in same shape as fish. Place fish, skin side down, on paste. Spread remaining paste on top of fish. Fold both sides of plastic wrap around fish, securing well, then fold in lengthwise pieces of plastic wrap. Securely tuck edges underneath the fish to seal it well. (If curing 2 or 3 sides of fish at the same time, you can stack them all in the same pan.)

3. Refrigerate at least 48 hours, or up to 72 hours for a more flavorful cure, flipping fish upside down every 12 hours. Be careful not to loosen plastic wrap when flipping the fish.

4. Remove fish from refrigerator, unwrap, and gently scrape off curing paste with a rubber spatula. Be careful not to tear the flesh. Rinse fish quickly in cold water to remove excess paste. Pat dry, cover with clean plastic wrap, and refrigerate flesh-side up for up to 5 days.

5. To serve, slice fish very thinly along the diagonal with a very sharp knife. To serve skinless fillets, first flip fish upside down and slice skin off the bottom in one piece. Arrange salmon on a platter and sprinkle with dill. Serve with toast, crackers, or rye bread.

TUNA TONNATO WITH ARUGULA ON GRILLED BREAD

Tonnato is a creamy tuna sauce with Italian roots that is traditionally served over cold sliced veal. Other than the veal stock in the sauce (you can substitute homemade brown chicken stock), I like to let the tuna take the spotlight in this lighter, salad-style dish. For a summer version, replace the tuna with peak-of-season sliced tomatoes.

—————— MAKES 8 APPETIZER SERVINGS, PLUS ADDITIONAL TONNATO SAUCE ——————

Tonnato Sauce

1 large egg yolk

1½ teaspoons sherry vinegar

1½ teaspoons freshly squeezed lemon juice

1 anchovy fillet, rinsed

1½ teaspoons capers, rinsed

1 (5-ounce) can water-packed tuna, drained

½ cup extra-virgin olive oil

½ cup Brown Veal Stock (*recipe page 194*) or Brown Chicken Stock (*recipe page 195*)

Crostini and Ahi Salad

4 slices rustic sourdough bread, sliced in half, or 8 smaller baguette slices

3 tablespoons extra-virgin olive oil, divided, more for drizzling

1 tablespoon Dijon mustard

1 tablespoon dark sesame oil

1 tablespoon fresh tarragon, chopped

2 (6-ounce) ahi tuna steaks, about ¾-inch thick

Coarse sea or kosher salt, to taste

2 cups baby arugula

1 teaspoon freshly squeezed lemon juice, more to taste

½ cup (about ½ pint) cherry, grape, or other small tomatoes, halved

Freshly ground pepper, to taste

1 tablespoon bonito flakes, optional

Lemon wedges, for serving

1. To make sauce, combine egg yolk, vinegar, lemon juice, anchovy, and capers in a blender and purée into a paste. Add tuna and olive oil and mix well. Add stock and mix again until it has a sauce-like texture.

2. To make crostini, brush bread with 1 tablespoon olive oil. In a stovetop grill pan, on the grill, or under a broiler, lightly toast bread on both sides. Set aside.

3. To make salad, in a small bowl, whisk together mustard, sesame oil, and tarragon. Rub tuna steaks on both sides with marinade and lightly sprinkle with salt. In a large sauté pan, heat 1 tablespoon olive oil over medium-high heat. When oil is hot, sear tuna steaks on both sides for about 1 minute for medium-rare, or to your liking. Remove from pan and slice thinly crosswise.

4. In a large bowl, toss arugula with lemon juice and remaining 1 tablespoon olive oil. To assemble crostini, generously spread tonnato sauce on each slice of toasted bread. Top with arugula and a few tomatoes and season with pepper to taste. Lay 3 to 4 slices of tuna on top of arugula and sprinkle with bonito flakes, if desired. Serve immediately with additional tonnato sauce and lemon wedges on the side.

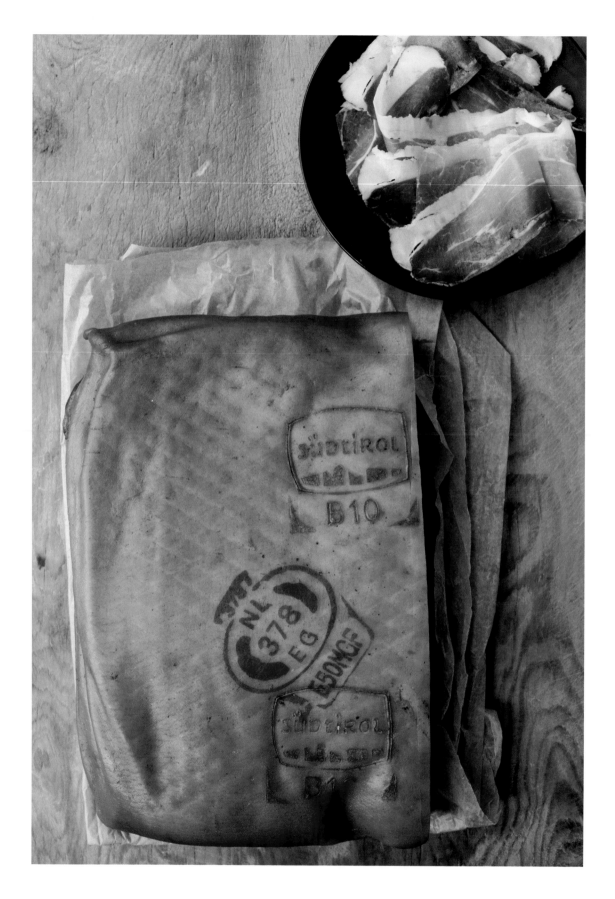

BLACK FOREST HAM PANINI

This grilled sandwich combines American-style "Black Forest" ham, a misnomer that applies to dry-cured, smoked deli hams, and authentic Black Forest ham, a really fantastic, prosciutto-like smoked and cured ham. A ham on ham sandwich, basically—well, depending on whom you ask.

MAKES 4 LARGE SANDWICHES OR 16 MINI COCKTAIL SANDWICHES

1. Divide mustard among 8 slices of bread. Top 4 slices bread with 1 slice of cheese and 1 piece American-style dry-cured ham. Divide onions among sandwiches and top each with a thin slice of Black Forest ham. Close with another mustard-covered slice of bread and press down firmly.

2. In a large sauté pan, heat 1 generous tablespoon butter over medium-high heat. When foam subsides, add 2 sandwiches and top with a heavy cast-iron skillet or other heavy pan to press sandwiches flat. Sauté until golden brown on one side, about 2 minutes. Flip sandwiches with a spatula, top again with a skillet, and continue to cook until well-toasted on opposite side, about 2 minutes. Wipe out pan with a paper towel and repeat with remaining butter and sandwiches. Slice sandwiches in half, or to make mini cocktail panini, slice in quarters, and serve immediately. If not serving immediately, keep warm for up to 20 minutes in a 200° oven.

3 tablespoons Dijon mustard, divided, or to taste

8 slices rye bread

8 thin slices gruyère cheese

4 ⅛th-inch-thick slices (12 ounces) American-style "Black Forest" dry-cured ham

1 cup Quick Caramelized Onions (*recipe page 200*)

4 paper-thin slices (about 2 ounces) authentic smoked Black Forest ham or Italian speck

About 2½ tablespoons unsalted butter, divided

Black Forest Ham

The smoked, American-style Black Forest ham you find at most deli counters is worlds apart from the real deal. The authentic version has a Protected Designation of Origin and can be made only in the Black Forest region of southwestern Germany, where I'm from. The ham is salt-cured and seasoned with coriander, juniper berries, and other spices, and allowed to air dry for several weeks. It's then cold-smoked with fir wood at a very low temperature, almost room temperature (less than 80°), for several weeks. The finished ham very closely resembles speck with a dark, smoky exterior. (Speck comes from the Alto Adige region of Italy, which borders Austria and Germany and produces many Germanic-inspired products.) Both are intensely flavored—a good thing, like aged salami—and should be sliced very thinly.

You can find the real thing at quality butcher shops and German delis, or online from such vendors as continentalsausage.com (the ham is called "American-style" when the exterior layer of fat has been removed), or substitute speck, which is more widely available online and at delis and grocery stores.

SMOKED TROUT CONSOMMÉ WITH DUMPLINGS

In Germany, trout has long been enjoyed fresh and in several preserved forms. That wasn't always the case in the United States. But now that quality farm-raised trout is commonly available at seafood markets, you can forgo the fishing trip once required for a fresh catch. Smoking the fish adds an incredibly rich flavor, so I like to serve the consommé in shallow bowls or small cups.

If you can't find whole smoked trout for the stock, ask your fishmonger for stock bones from fresh trout or a similar whitefish and add a few smoked trout fillets. Other flaky smoked white fish, such as haddock, also work well.

MAKES 8 STARTER SERVINGS

1. To make consommé, if using whole trout, debone and fillet the fish, reserving skin, bones, fins, head, and tail. Finely chop about 3 tablespoons each of the roughly chopped carrots, parsnips, and celery root or stalks, and set aside.

2. In a medium stockpot, combine 6 cups water, wine, remaining roughly chopped carrots, parsnips, and celery root or stalks, onion, bay leaf, peppercorns, fennel, coriander, salt, and smoked trout carcass (or smoked trout fillets and stock bones). Bring to a very low boil (do not vigorously boil), reduce heat, and simmer over medium-low heat for 30 minutes. Remove from heat. When cool enough to handle, strain consommé, discard solids, and return to pot. Season with salt and pepper to taste. Bring to a simmer, reduce heat to low, and add reserved finely diced carrot, celery root, and parsnip. Set aside while you prepare the dumplings.

3. To make dumplings, crumble bread into very small pieces into a small bowl. Add consommé and mix together with your fingers.

4. In a medium bowl, combine softened butter, lemon zest, nutmeg, salt, egg yolks, and flaked trout and mix well with your fingers or a rubber spatula. (If using an 8-ounce package of smoked trout, reserve remaining 6 ounces for soup garnish.) Add chives, soaked bread, breadcrumbs, and 1 tablespoon flour and mix well. Mixture will be very moist.

(continued)

Consommé

2 whole smoked trout (about 1½ pounds each), cleaned

or

16 ounces smoked trout fillets plus 1 pound fresh trout or other whitefish bones

2 medium carrots, peeled and roughly chopped

2 small parsnips, peeled and roughly chopped

½ large celery root, peeled, or 2 medium stalks celery, roughly chopped

1 cup dry white wine, such as Sauvignon Blanc

1 large onion, sliced in half

1 bay leaf

1 teaspoon black peppercorns

1 teaspoon fennel seeds

1 teaspoon coriander seeds

1 teaspoon coarse sea or kosher salt, more to taste

White pepper, to taste

Trout Dumplings

1 slice day-old white sandwich-style bread, crusts removed

2 tablespoons trout consommé

6 tablespoons (3 ounces) unsalted butter, room temperature

Zest of ½ medium lemon

Pinch nutmeg

Pinch coarse sea or kosher salt, more to taste

2 large egg yolks

¼ of 8-ounce package (2 ounces or about ¼ cup) smoked trout fillets, skinned and boned (reserve remaining 6 ounces for soup)

1 tablespoon finely chopped chives

½ cup unseasoned, dry bread-crumbs (*recipe page 21*)

4 tablespoons flour, divided

To serve

6 ounces smoked trout, flaked

2 tablespoons finely chopped chives

5. Place remaining 3 tablespoons flour in a small bowl. Roughly shape trout mixture into 8 balls, and roll each in flour, passing the dumplings back and forth between the palms of your hands a few times to form a firm ball. Set aside on a plate.

6. Fill a medium pot halfway with water, bring to a boil, reduce to a simmer, and carefully drop half of dumplings into water (to avoid breaking dumplings, do not allow water to return to a boil). Simmer, uncovered, until firm, about 10 minutes, flipping each after 5 minutes to evenly cook the top (the dumplings float). Use slotted spoon to transfer dumplings to a clean plate. Repeat with remaining dumplings. Allow to cool for 5 minutes and use a serrated knife to gently cut each into 3 to 4 slices. Alternatively, serve dumplings whole.

7. To serve, re-warm consommé over medium heat until hot and divide among 8 shallow soup bowls. Sprinkle remaining 6 ounces of flaked trout and place 1 whole dumpling or 2 to 3 slices of dumplings in soup. Top with chives and serve immediately.

Marinara

FENNEL SAUSAGE IN MARINARA

This vegetable-packed marinara is the root of most of my tomato-based dishes. The fennel sausage meatballs (see recipe page 52) that I lucked into from a Chicago butcher beg for a big hunk of crusty bread to sop up the sauce, pasta optional. Or spear some mini meatballs on toothpicks for a little retro, stammtisch-hour party fun. Either way, a meatball sub the next day is a must.

MAKES 5 TO 6 MAIN COURSE SERVINGS, OR 8 TO 10 COCKTAIL SERVINGS

1. To make marinara, heat olive oil in a large saucepan or Dutch oven over medium-high heat. Add onion, carrots, and garlic and cook until vegetables are softened and just beginning to brown, 5 to 7 minutes. Smash tomatoes with your fingers and add to pot with juices, scraping up any brown bits on bottom of pan. Add bay leaf, salt, and pepper and simmer for 30 minutes, stirring occasionally. Stir in fresh oregano and season with pepper to taste. Avoid over-seasoning with salt at this point; the salt in the sausages will flavor the sauce. Use immediately, or refrigerate for up to 3 days, or freeze.

2. To make meatballs, shape sausages into about 24 1-inch balls, pressing together firmly but gently so they hold together but are not overly packed. Heat olive oil in a large sauté pan over medium-high heat. Fry half of meatballs until golden brown on one side, about 3 to 4 minutes. Flip once and repeat on opposite side (do not flip more often or they will fall apart). Transfer cooked meatballs to Dutch oven with warm marinara. Repeat with remaining meatballs.

3. Bring marinara to a simmer, reduce heat to low, cover, and slowly cook until meatballs are tender, about 30 minutes. Season with salt and pepper to taste, and sprinkle with parmesan. Serve immediately with crusty bread.

Marinara

3 tablespoons extra-virgin olive oil

½ large yellow onion, finely chopped

2 carrots, peeled and finely chopped

5 medium cloves garlic, minced

1 (28-ounce) can whole tomatoes, preferably San Marzano

1 bay leaf

Generous pinch coarse sea or kosher salt, more to taste

½ teaspoon freshly ground pepper, more to taste

2 tablespoons fresh oregano leaves, chopped

Meatballs and serving

1 pound Fennel Sausage (*recipe page 52*)

1 tablespoon extra-virgin olive oil

Freshly grated parmesan, for serving

Plenty of crusty bread, for serving

SPRECHEN SIE SUPPER?

THE COMFORTS OF MY GERMAN HOME

Comfort foods like spätzle, schnitzel, and goulash remind me the most of home. At some point, I'm pretty sure I've slipped every single dish I've ever craved onto my menus—a handy prerogative for chefs.

Most were popular with my customers and still are today. But I was always surprised when a few of my childhood favorites didn't go over well. In Germany, organ meats like calf's liver are a delicacy. I love the textural contrast, the brown-butter-like toasty exterior and rich, earthy center. But back when I had the restaurant Röckenwagner, every time I tried to work a dish into my menu rotation like *kalbsleber Berliner art*, Berlin-style calf's liver seared with apples and onions, few people ordered it. My staff and I would eat very well those weeks.

I suspect that today, those old Röckenwagner menus would meet with more success among today's more globally sophisticated eaters. What we put on the dinner table at home has also changed. Dinner is often the one time we have to sit down with family and friends, to enjoy a long, or at least longer, meal the way our grandparents did over lunch. Heartier dishes like grilled flank steak and potatoes, or maybe a whole roast chicken with several vegetable sides, restore us after a long day. And we all still have those nights when we crave a classic, warming spätzle dish.

With so many fresh ingredients available literally at our doorsteps, we can play around in the kitchen so much more today than people could in our grandparents' day. When I put a monkfish version of sauerbraten, the classic beef pot roast with a vinegar marinade, on my first restaurant menu years ago, it was seen as noteworthy among critics. Chefs didn't always step outside the unspoken parameters of their regional cuisine. Now, cooking more creatively is not only expected but is something many of us enjoy doing at home. More recently, even my jägerschnitzel ("hunter's-style" pork schnitzel) has subtly morphed into a version speckled with fresh market vegetables and a little less cream. Granted, it's not cream-free. Let's not get carried away.

WARM BRUSSELS SPROUTS & KALE SALAD
WITH BLUE CHEESE DRESSING

We serve this warm salad for lunch at 3 Square Café, but it can also serve as a two-veggies-in-one dinner side. Or add some bread and you've got a light vegetarian supper.

For the sauce, use a mild, creamy blue cheese like bavarian, saga, or cambozola, a German cross between creamy camembert and gorgonzola. American-style cheeses like Maytag Blue are too strong on their own and need to be tamed with a little goat cheese.

MAKES 6 SIDE SERVINGS

1. In a large sauté pan, heat olive oil over medium-high heat. Add brussels sprouts and sauté until beginning to brown, stirring occasionally, about 5 minutes. Add 1 cup water, bring to a simmer, and cook until brussels sprouts are crisp-tender, 2 to 3 minutes if sprouts are very small, up to 6 to 8 minutes if larger. Add cheese, stir to melt, and then add kale. Continue to cook until kale has just wilted, about 30 seconds. Stir in lemon juice.

2. Remove pan from heat and season with salt, pepper, and additional lemon juice to taste. Sprinkle with pine nuts and pomegranate seeds, if desired, and serve immediately.

2 tablespoons extra-virgin olive oil

1½ pounds brussels sprouts, cut in half if small, quartered if large

6 ounces mild, creamy blue cheese, or 4 ounces goat cheese and 2 ounces strong, crumbly blue cheese

1 small bunch kale, stemmed and roughly chopped

1 tablespoon freshly squeezed lemon juice, more to taste

Coarse sea or kosher salt and freshly ground pepper, to taste

3 tablespoons lightly toasted pine nuts (*see page 193*)

2 tablespoons pomegranate seeds, optional

MUSSEL CHOWDER WITH PARSNIPS & LEEKS

Parsnips, which were used to sweeten dishes in medieval Europe, have a subtle sweetness and earthy flavor that really complement mussels.

MAKES 4 SERVINGS AS A LIGHT SUPPER

½ pound parsnips (about 2 medium or 1 small bunch baby parsnips), peeled and cored if large (see page 190)

2 tablespoons (1 ounce) unsalted butter

1 medium shallot, finely chopped

1 medium leek, white part only, finely chopped

1 medium clove garlic, minced

1 bay leaf

3 sprigs dill, divided

½ teaspoon coarse sea or kosher salt, more to taste

½ teaspoon freshly ground pepper, more to taste

¼ cup dry white wine

2 pounds mussels, beards removed and well scrubbed

1 cup heavy cream

Small handful parsley leaves

Plenty of crusty bread, for serving

1. Finely chop parsnips into roughly ¼-inch pieces. Fill a medium saucepan ⅓ full of water. Bring to a simmer over medium-high heat, add parsnips, cover, and cook until just tender, 5 to 7 minutes. Strain, and rinse parsnips under cold water for a minute or two to partially cool. Set aside.

2. In a large Dutch oven or heavy-bottomed stockpot, heat butter over medium heat. When foam subsides, add shallot, leek, garlic, bay leaf, 1 sprig dill, salt, and pepper and cook, stirring occasionally, until vegetables are softened, about 4 to 5 minutes. Deglaze pan with wine, increase heat to medium-high, and cook until wine is slightly reduced, about 1 minute. Add 1½ cups water and bring to a low boil. Add mussels, cover, and cook until mussels open, 4 to 5 minutes. Add cream and parsnips, cook 30 seconds longer to warm, and turn off heat. Season broth with additional salt and pepper to taste.

3. Meanwhile, finely chop remaining 2 sprigs dill and parsley leaves. Divide mussels and broth among wide soup bowls and sprinkle with herbs. Discard any mussels that do not open. Serve immediately with crusty bread.

SCHNITZEL

Many Americans think of schnitzel as a specific dish, usually veal or chicken, that is pounded thin, breaded, and pan-fried. That version, which is very good, is called *wiener schnitzel*, or Viennese-style schnitzel.

But in Germany, schnitzel is a broad category for the way meat is cut. The word literally means "cutlets." There are countless variations using different types of meat and all sorts of preparations (even a "natural" schnitzel, meaning naked with no breadcrumbs), and sauces, from cream to tomato-based.

HOW TO POUND MEAT FOR SCHNITZEL

Place 1 veal, chicken, or pork cutlet at a time in a large food storage bag (do not seal) or between 2 pieces of waxed paper. Bang meat with a heavy skillet or the flat side of a meat pounder until about ⅛-inch thick. It should be almost doubled or more in size, depending on original size and thickness of meat.

• Never pound a thin cutlet with the ridged, tenderizing side of a meat pounder. It breaks up the meat. Use the flat side of the pounder or a heavy pan, like an iron skillet.

• Buy a better cut of meat, especially when you are cooking boneless chicken breasts or pork. Go to a good butcher and ask for ½-inch-thick cutlets about 5 inches long.

• Meat at many grocery stores today is inconsistent in size, particularly chicken and pork. Look for boneless pork chops or chicken breasts labeled "thin cut" or those cut less than ½-inch thick. If you can find only very thick cuts, slice the meat in half lengthwise through the middle before pounding.

• When in doubt, keep pounding. Thickness depends on the dish. Typically, cutlets should be about ⅛-inch thick. If some of the meat tears, just bread and fry the smaller pieces.

WIENER SCHNITZEL

Regular butter is always good, but for the ultimate classic wiener schnitzel, use clarified butter. To make quick work of leftovers, if you're lucky enough to have any, slice the meat and use it instead of roasted chicken in salads or sandwiches.

MAKES 4 SERVINGS

1. Preheat oven to 200°. Line a baking sheet with paper towels.

2. Season both sides of cutlets lightly with salt. Place flour in a small bowl. In another small bowl, lightly beat eggs. Spread out breadcrumbs in a shallow bowl or large plate.

3. Dip cutlets into flour, coating both sides, and then dip into egg, gently shaking off excess egg. Dredge well in breadcrumbs, lightly patting with your hands to adhere, and set aside at room temperature for 10 minutes.

4. In a large, heavy-bottomed skillet, heat 2 tablespoons butter over medium-high heat. When foam subsides, add 1 or 2 cutlets (to fit in pan without overcrowding), and sauté until golden brown on one side, 3 to 4 minutes. Flip, and cook on opposite side until no longer pink in the center, about 2 minutes, depending on thickness. Transfer to baking sheet and place in oven to keep warm.

5. Carefully wipe out hot pan with paper towels. Repeat frying process as needed with remaining cutlets. Sprinkle schnitzel with parsley and season with salt to taste. Serve immediately with lemon wedges.

1¼ pounds chicken or veal cutlets (4 large or 8 small fillets), pounded about ⅛-inch thick

Coarse sea or kosher salt, to taste

¾ cup flour

2 large eggs

1½ cups unseasoned fine, dry breadcrumbs (*recipe page 21*)

6 to 8 tablespoons unsalted or clarified butter, divided

Chopped flat-leaf parsley, to taste

Lemon wedges, for serving

JÄGERSCHNITZEL

Jägerschnitzel, or "hunter's schnitzel," has always been one of my favorites. I wrap my version of this classic dish in prosciutto-like Black Forest ham (see page 101) *to give it a nice, meaty crust.*

Pound the chops a little thicker, more like ½ inch (don't worry about the bone—just focus your pounding on the meat) and use whatever market-fresh onions and mushrooms you find.

———— MAKES 4 SERVINGS ————

1. Season the chops lightly on both sides with salt and pepper. Wrap 2 slices ham around the middle of each chop like a package, covering most of the meat. Lightly press together edges to seal and dip each chop in flour to coat both sides, shaking to remove excess.

2. In a large, heavy-bottomed skillet, heat 1 tablespoon olive oil over medium-high heat. Add 2 chops and sauté until golden brown on one side, 3 to 4 minutes. Flip and cook another 2 to 3 minutes to brown opposite side. Transfer to a plate and repeat with remaining tablespoon of olive oil and remaining chops.

3. Add shallots and garlic to same pan and sauté over medium heat until just beginning to brown, 2 to 3 minutes. Add spring or pearl onions and mushrooms and cook until mushrooms begin to soften, 4 to 5 minutes. Deglaze with wine, scraping up any brown bits on bottom of pan, and cook until wine almost evaporates, about 2 minutes. Add veal or chicken stock, bring to a simmer, and return pork chops and drippings to pan. Continue to cook over medium heat until chops are only slightly pink in center, flipping once, about 3 to 5 minutes, depending on thickness. Place chops on serving plates and use a slotted spoon to transfer vegetables on top (a few smaller vegetables can remain in pan).

4. Heat remaining jus to a simmer and whisk in butter followed by a splash of cream. Season sauce with salt and pepper and sprinkle parsley on top. Spoon sauce over chops and serve immediately.

4 (1-inch-thick) bone-in pork chops (5 to 6 ounces each), pounded for schnitzel to about ½-inch thick

Coarse sea or kosher salt, to taste

Freshly ground pepper, to taste

8 paper-thin slices Black Forest ham or speck

⅓ cup flour

2 tablespoons extra-virgin olive oil, divided

2 shallots, finely diced

4 medium cloves garlic, sliced in half

1 bunch spring onions, trimmed, or ½ cup pearl onions, peeled

2 cups mixed mushrooms, such as chanterelle, oyster, and/or shiitake

¼ cup dry white wine

½ cup Brown Veal Stock (*recipe page 194*) or Brown Chicken Stock (*recipe page 195*), warmed

2 tablespoons (1 ounce) unsalted butter, chilled

Generous splash heavy cream

¼ cup chopped parsley

SCHWEINEFLEISCH

Germans have long appreciated *schwein* (pork): chops, roasts, tenderloin, bacon, ham, sausage, head cheese—truly the whole hog.

In Germany, pork has long been prepared to make the most of every last bite—whether cured, pâté-style, ground into meatloaves, or as *wursts* (sausages). Cuts popular with chefs today, like pork belly, were once the more humble "off" cuts. You could buy them inexpensively with other full-flavored, marbled cuts to grind up into sausages for another day. You never threw any part of the animal away, a trend that I'm glad to see we're getting back to today.

The pig eventually became a Teutonic symbol of good fortune. Pork and sauerkraut is typically eaten on New Year's Day, much like the black-eyed pea tradition in the South, and tiny marzipan piglets are given as tokens of good luck. Referring to someone as a "lucky pig" means they've come upon good fortune.

My father was a butcher, so we had plenty of good luck in getting the best cuts of meat: like big, hearty chops, delicate tenderloins, and juicy roasts. Most Sundays, he would cook up a roast of some kind for lunch. My favorite was his cut of pork neck. I can still taste it. It was a well-marbled portion of meat with just the right fat ratio to get a crackling crust and tender, incredibly moist hunks of meat. I compare every cut of *schweinefleisch* that comes into my kitchen to his.

LAMB BURGERS WITH JALAPEÑO RAISIN CHUTNEY

I suppose these lamb burgers are the California cousins of frikadellen (see "Hamburger," page 73), the German version of meatballs made with day-old bread and shaped like patties. This meat mixture also makes fantastic meatballs when dunked in homemade marinara (recipe page 105).

To keep the moist patties from sticking, oil the grill and your spatula well. And if you're a diehard rare or medium-rare fan, keep in mind that with so many ingredients, you still need to cook the burgers a little longer. You can dress these burgers any way you'd like, but if you have some of the chutney in the fridge, it's pretty hard to beat that.

——————————————— MAKES 4 BURGERS ———————————————

1½ teaspoons fennel seeds

1 tablespoon extra-virgin olive oil

¼ large onion, minced

1 medium clove garlic, minced

¼ cup whole milk

1 cup roughly chopped day-old brioche or other white bread (about 1 medium slice), crusts removed

1 large egg

1 tablespoon sweet paprika

½ teaspoon crushed red pepper flakes, more to taste

1 teaspoon coarse sea or kosher salt

1 pound ground lamb

Vegetable oil, for grill

4 tablespoons Jalapeño Raisin Chutney (*recipe page 197*)

4 small pretzel buns (*recipe page 20*) or good-quality store-bought buns, lightly toasted and buttered

2 medium roasted red bell peppers, seeded and quartered (*see page 193*), or jarred peppers, drained

1. Heat a small pan over medium-high heat. Add fennel seeds and toast until fragrant and just beginning to color, 1½ to 2 minutes, shaking the pan often. Transfer to a medium bowl.

2. In a medium saucepan, heat olive oil over medium heat. Add onion and garlic and sauté until softened, stirring occasionally, 3 to 4 minutes, and turn off heat. Add milk and bread, stirring in bread until well combined. Set aside to cool for 5 minutes.

3. Add egg, paprika, red pepper flakes, and salt to bowl with fennel seeds and mix well to combine. When cool enough to handle, break up any large chunks of soaked bread and pour over egg mixture. Add lamb and gently mix with your fingers until well incorporated. Chill at least 30 minutes, preferably 1 hour or more.

4. Prepare a charcoal or gas grill for direct grilling over medium-high heat. Form meat into 4 4-inch patties. Brush grill surface generously with vegetable oil. Use a lightly oiled spatula to gently transfer burgers to grill and cook, covered, until meat just begins to feel firm to the touch, about 6 to 8 minutes. Oil spatula, gently flip burgers, and continue to grill, uncovered, until firm to the touch (medium to medium-well), 5 to 7 minutes.

5. Spread Jalapeño Raisin Chutney on buns. Place a lamb patty on each bun and top with few slices of bell pepper. Serve immediately.

Lamb Meatballs in Marinara

To make these, use the same recipe as for the lamb burgers. After chilling the lamb mixture, divide it in half. Form each half into 8 meatballs, packing each firmly together. Refrigerate for 30 minutes to 1 hour. In a large saucepan, heat 1 tablespoon extra-virgin olive oil over medium-high heat and sauté half of meatballs until golden brown on all sides, 6 to 8 minutes. Transfer to a plate and repeat with remaining meatballs. Drain most of fat from pan, add Marinara (*see recipe page 105*), and bring sauce to a simmer. Transfer meatballs to sauce and cook, loosely covered, until tender, about 30 minutes. Sprinkle with parmesan and chopped parsley, and serve over pasta or with crusty bread. Makes 4 to 6 servings.

JIDORI BRICK CHICKEN

Jidori is a free-range Japanese chicken made popular by Los Angeles chefs ever since a local farmer began raising them. It has a very clean, pure chicken flavor that really stands out in this citrusy marinade. I love to serve this dish with the Lemony Potatoes (see recipe page 135).

You can find Jidori chicken increasingly at specialty butchers, or substitute any good-quality chicken from the farmers' market. Keep in mind that Jidori tend to be small and lean, with little added water. If you substitute another variety, you may need to cook the bird longer.

MAKES 4 TO 6 SERVINGS

1½ tablespoons coarse sea or kosher salt

1 tablespoon sugar

1½ large lemons, divided

2 small Jidori chickens, about 3 pounds each

½ cup Dijon mustard

1 medium clove garlic, minced

1½ teaspoons fresh tarragon leaves

1½ teaspoons fresh thyme leaves

½ teaspoon coarse sea or kosher salt

½ teaspoon finely ground pepper, preferably white

3 tablespoons extra-virgin olive oil, divided

Lemony Potatoes (*recipe page 135*), optional

1. In a large bowl or food container, combine 6 cups water, salt, and sugar. Thinly slice 1 lemon and add to brine. Set aside.

2. To cut chicken in half, slice alongside and through both sides of backbone and breastbone so legs and breast are still attached to each other. (Save bones for stock.) Trim off excess fat and add chicken to brine. Cover and refrigerate for 12 to 24 hours.

3. Discard brine, including lemons. Pat chicken and bowl dry and return chicken to bowl.

4. In a small bowl, mix together mustard, garlic, tarragon, thyme, salt, pepper, 1 tablespoon olive oil, and zest and juice of remaining ½ lemon. Spread seasoned mustard over chicken, inside and out, cover, and refrigerate for at least 2 or up to 6 hours.

5. Remove chicken from refrigerator 1 hour before cooking. Preheat oven to 400°. Wrap two bricks in aluminum foil. If you don't have bricks, wrap bottom of another heavy skillet in foil.

6. Heat a large, heavy-bottomed, and oven-proof skillet (to fit both birds) over medium-high heat for 2 minutes and add 1 tablespoon olive oil. Dab 1 chicken lightly with a paper towel and place in skillet, skin-side down. Place foil-covered bricks, or a foil-wrapped skillet with 2 heavy cans (28-ounce tomato cans work well), on top of chicken. Cook until skin is dark golden brown, 12 to 16 minutes. Be careful when checking not to tear skin; use a spatula to "scrape" up chicken with skin attached. Transfer to a plate and repeat with remaining oil and chicken. Discard marinade.

7. Remove bricks or skillet, return all chicken to pan, skin-side up, and place in oven. Roast, uncovered, until juices run clear, 10 to 14 minutes for small birds, longer for larger birds. Remove from oven and allow to rest for 5 minutes. Spoon pan juices over chicken and serve immediately.

MAC 'N' CHEESE SOUFFLÉ

My parents owned a restaurant that they would close for a week or two each summer to go on vacation in Spain or Italy. This would leave me, a teenager, in charge of watching over an empty restaurant with a fully stocked pantry. I loved making big pots of pasta to share with my friends. (I will refrain from commenting on whether anything was shared from the wine cellar.) To this day, pasta is the one food I could not go without.

The marinara served with this lighter, almost soufflé-like version of mac 'n' cheese really pulls the flavors together.

───────────────── MAKES 4 SOUFFLÉS ─────────────────

1. Preheat oven to 375°. Generously butter 4 16-ounce soufflé dishes.

2. Place 1 baking dish large enough to fit all soufflé dishes, in the oven or use 2 medium dishes. Fill with about 2 inches of water.

3. In a medium sauté pan, melt 2 tablespoons butter over medium-high heat. When foam subsides, add breadcrumbs and toast until golden brown, about 3 to 4 minutes, stirring often. Remove from heat.

4. In a medium saucepan, melt remaining 2 tablespoons butter over medium heat. Add flour, whisk to incorporate, and cook until just beginning to color, 1 to 1½ minutes. Slowly add milk, whisking constantly. Cook until sauce is thickened, 2 to 3 minutes, whisking occasionally. Remove from heat, add all three cheeses, and stir until melted. Season with cayenne and set aside.

5. When sauce has cooled slightly, transfer to a large bowl. Whisk in 2 egg yolks, add macaroni, and stir well to coat pasta.

6. In a stand mixer fitted with the whisk attachment, beat 5 egg whites on high until they hold peaks but are not dry, about 3 to 4 minutes. Fold ⅓ of whites into pasta and mix well. Fold second ⅓ of whites into pasta more gently. With final ⅓, fold until just combined; some white flecks should remain.

7. Immediately divide batter between 4 buttered soufflé dishes and top each with toasted breadcrumbs. Place in water bath and reduce temperature to 350°. Bake until soufflés have risen and begin to brown on top, 25 to 28 minutes.

8. Meanwhile, warm marinara in a small saucepan. Serve soufflés immediately with marinara sauce on the side to spoon on top.

4 tablespoons unsalted butter, divided, more for coating dishes

½ cup unseasoned, toasted bread-crumbs (*recipe page 21*)

2 tablespoons flour

1¼ cups whole milk

¾ cup grated cheddar, packed

¾ cup grated fontina, packed

½ cup grated gruyère, packed

Generous pinch cayenne pepper, more to taste

2 large eggs, separated, at room temperature for 30 minutes

6 ounces macaroni, cooked al dente and rinsed under cold water (about 3 cups, cooked)

3 large egg whites, at room temperature for 30 minutes

½ cup Marinara (*recipe page 105*)

SPÄTZLE

Spätzle are a staple in southern Germany. The dumpling-like noodles are essentially the German equivalent of homemade pasta, only much more forgiving. The entire point is to make noodles that are not uniformly shaped for textural contrast. You'll find short and stubby *knöpfle* ("little buttons"), more delicate long strands, and every shape in between.

Every cook in Germany has a preferred technique for shaping spätzle, with all kinds of gadgets to help you. My favorite method? The old-fashioned way: by hand.

SHAPING SPÄTZLE

Spätzle press or potato ricer: A spätzle press looks like a giant potato ricer or garlic press. You put the dough in the chamber, and then squeeze the dough out the opposite end into boiling water. A ricer also works well, but don't use a food mill with a grinding plate. It compresses the dough.

A spätzle grater, box grater, or colander: With the soft, almost batter-like texture of the dough, using a spätzle grater or the large holes on a box grater can be trickier to master but works well once you get the hang of it. Some people also swear by the colander method. You press the dough through a colander (not a fine-mesh strainer) with medium holes. The only trick is finding a colander with the right-size holes. They need to be about ¼-inch wide.

Handmade spätzle: Making noodles by hand means the batter is never compressed, so the noodles are lighter and have more surface texture. It's also very easy to do, just quickly "shave" small flecks of dough into the boiling water to make the noodles. You can use a traditional spätzle board and scraper, which is a small wooden board along with a tool similar to a bench or pastry scraper. A small cutting board and a pastry scraper or offset spatula also work well.

CLASSIC SPÄTZLE

Make the dumpling-like noodles a day ahead, and dinner takes all of a matter of minutes: Just sauté the boiled spätzle in butter and top with parsley or whatever chopped herbs you prefer. To vary the dough, add a few tablespoons of fresh herbs or small seeds like caraway, poppy, or sesame.

If you've never made spätzle, scraping and boiling the noodles is really very easy after that initial test run. The dough is very moist, almost like thick pancake batter. Small wooden cutting boards work best, but if you have only a large, heavy wood board, a plastic board can be easier to hold over the water. Just be sure to wrap a kitchen towel around the handle of the pot to avoid melting it.

MAKES 4 SERVINGS

1. In a medium bowl, whisk together flour, ½ teaspoon salt, and nutmeg. Make a well in the center of the flour, break eggs into the middle, and add about half of the milk. Use a fork or wooden spoon to incorporate eggs by beating in a circular motion. Gradually incorporate flour toward center with eggs first, then flour toward the outer edges, as you would making pasta. As the batter becomes dry, add remaining half of milk, continuing to beat in same motion. The mixture should look like thick pancake batter and have few lumps. Let dough rest for 10 minutes while you bring water to a boil.

2. Fill a large bowl with cold water and ice. Fill a large pot halfway with water, add remaining 1 teaspoon salt, and bring to a boil. Snugly wrap a kitchen towel around one handle of the pot, being careful that the towel is not close to the flame.

3. Just before cooking, beat dough with a fork or spoon a few times to aerate. Scoop out about ⅓ of dough with a ladle or measuring cup and place on the end of a spätzle board or medium cutting board. Loosely shape dough into a long rectangle about 4 inches wide. Rest cutting board on kitchen towel over boiling water. Use a spätzle scraper, pastry scraper, or blunt knife to quickly scrape thin ribbons of dough off the board and into the water. Shake scraper or knife above water if necessary to "flick" off dough. (Don't shave dough pieces too large or spätzle will fall apart as it boils). If batter spreads out to edges of cutting board, use the scraper to guide it back toward the center.

(continued)

2 cups flour

1½ teaspoons coarse sea or kosher salt, divided, more to taste

Pinch of freshly ground nutmeg

6 large eggs

½ cup whole milk

4 tablespoons (2 ounces) unsalted butter, divided

2 tablespoons chopped parsley, basil, or mixed fresh herbs

Freshly ground pepper, to taste

4. By the time you finish scraping dough (30 to 45 seconds), spätzle should have risen to the top of the water. With a long-handled skimmer, immediately transfer spätzle to ice bath. Bring water in pot back to a boil, and repeat with remaining batter. Strain spätzle from ice bath, gently shake to remove excess water, and transfer to a food storage container for up to 2 days.

5. When ready to serve, heat a large, preferably nonstick skillet over medium-high heat. Add 2 tablespoons butter, heat until foam begins to subside, and add half of spätzle. Sauté until beginning to turn golden brown in spots, about 2 minutes. Carefully flip and brown on the opposite side another 2 to 3 minutes. Transfer to a serving bowl and repeat with remaining butter and spätzle. Toss with parsley, season with salt and pepper to taste, and serve immediately.

SPRING SPÄTZLE WITH HERBS & PEAS

Spätzle was the first dish I learned to make as a teenager when my parents enlisted me to help at their restaurant. I don't know if I gravitated toward this chore because I disliked the other duties (such as cleaning the parking lot and taking out the trash), but I came to really enjoy making these handmade dumplings, which I did day in and day out by the potful. Over time, it became a source of pride as my spätzle became the base for which the restaurant's "real" chefs would create seasonal specials—like this one.

_____ MAKES 4 SERVINGS _____

6 tablespoons (3 ounces) unsalted butter, divided

1 large shallot, minced

2 bulbs green garlic (also known as spring garlic), including 1 inch of tender stem, roots trimmed and thinly sliced

1 cup fresh morels, cleaned and sliced in half if large

1 cup enoki mushrooms, whole, or small button mushrooms, sliced in half

½ cup freshly shelled English peas

1 medium bunch green asparagus, trimmed and cut into 1-inch pieces

Coarse sea or kosher salt, to taste

Spätzle (*recipe page 123*), boiled but not sautéed

½ cup heavy cream

Small handful pea shoots, leaves and tendrils only, or substitute basil leaves

Freshly ground pepper, to taste

1. In a large saucepan or Dutch oven, heat 2 tablespoons butter over medium-high heat. Add shallots and green garlic and sauté until just tender, 2 to 3 minutes. Add mushrooms and continue to cook until beginning to soften, 3 to 4 minutes. Add peas and asparagus and cook until crisp-tender, 4 to 5 minutes. Season with salt to taste and set aside.

2. In a large nonstick skillet, heat 2 tablespoons butter over medium-high heat until foam begins to subside, and add half of boiled spätzle. Sauté until beginning to turn golden brown in spots, about 2 minutes. Carefully flip and brown on the opposite side another 2 to 3 minutes. Transfer to pot with vegetables and repeat with remaining 2 tablespoons of butter and spätzle.

3. Add cream to spätzle and vegetables and heat until just warm, about 2 to 3 minutes. Sprinkle with pea shoots or basil and season with salt and pepper to taste. Serve immediately.

SHORT RIB GOULASH

This is an adaptation of my father's rindergulasch *(beef goulash), which he regularly made for weekend lunches. My version calls for bone-in short ribs, and I add lemon zest at the very end to brighten the flavors. It is best served with* spätzle *(see recipe page 123), but wide noodles also work.*

The short ribs at most grocery stores are typically less meaty than butcher shop bones. If you have a few lean ribs, brown and toss them into the pot anyway for flavor. You can fish them out later.

MAKES 6 SERVINGS, WITH LEFTOVERS

1. Season short ribs generously with salt. In a large Dutch oven or heavy-bottomed pot, heat oil over high heat. Sauté short ribs in two or three batches until well browned on all sides, 10 to 12 minutes. Do not crowd the pan or rush this step; browning is key to a good flavor. Transfer to a plate and repeat with remaining ribs. If needed to sear final batch, drain some of accumulated fat in pan so just a few tablespoons remain.

2. Drain off all but a thin, ¼-inch layer of fat. Reduce heat to medium, add onion and carrots, and sauté until vegetables begin to caramelize, about 8 to 10 minutes, stirring occasionally. Stir in garlic, paprika, coriander, cayenne, black pepper, and remaining ½ teaspoon salt. Cook for 30 seconds, add flour, and continue to cook, stirring frequently, for 2 minutes. Slowly add 2 cups beef or chicken stock, stirring constantly to scrape up any brown bits. Add tomato paste, stir well to combine, then add remaining 6 cups stock, vinegar, thyme, and bay leaves.

3. Return short ribs and any accumulated juices to pot. Bring to a boil, reduce heat, and gently simmer, uncovered, until short ribs are very tender, 2½ to 3 hours. Occasionally skim foam that rises to top and scrape bottom of pot to avoid burning. Allow goulash to cool completely, cover pot, and refrigerate overnight.

4. Remove goulash from refrigerator and skim off most of fat accumulated on top (leaving a bit is fine) and add lemon zest. Let rest at room temperature for a few hours before reheating, if possible (reheating the cold stew quickly makes it burn more easily on the bottom). Warm goulash over medium heat, covered, until warm, about 30 minutes. Stir occasionally, gently scraping bottom of pot, but try not to dislodge rib meat from bones.

5. Meanwhile, cook noodles according to package instructions and toss with butter. Season goulash with salt and pepper to taste and serve family-style.

4½ to 5 pounds meaty, bone-in beef short ribs

½ teaspoon coarse sea or kosher salt, more to season ribs and to taste

1 tablespoon vegetable oil

1 large onion, diced

2 medium carrots, peeled and diced

4 medium cloves garlic, minced

¼ cup sweet paprika

1 teaspoon ground coriander

¼ teaspoon cayenne pepper, or to taste

1 teaspoon freshly ground pepper, more to taste

⅓ cup flour

8 cups (64 ounces) low-sodium beef or chicken broth, divided

2 (6-ounce) cans (about 1¼ cups) tomato paste

2 tablespoons red wine vinegar

1 tablespoon fresh thyme leaves

2 bay leaves

To serve

2 teaspoons finely grated lemon zest

1 (12-ounce) package egg noodles (2 packages if eager noodle fans are present)

2 tablespoons unsalted butter

KOREAN FLANK STEAK WITH DAIKON
KIMCHEE & GERMAN POTATO SALAD

When it comes to meat, Germans are notoriously outspoken sugar-free cooks. Marriage has a way of mitigating these kinds of things. When I first tasted my mother-in-law's version of Korean flank steak, I loved how a little sugar really amplified the flavors and gave the meat a dark, caramelized sear.

Korean restaurants always serve kimchee (here, more of a crunchy salad-like version than the slow-fermented classic) as part of banchan, *the endless small sides that make appearances throughout a meal. You'll also usually find some kind of potato-based banchan, so at home, I like to serve my German-style potato salad* (see page 80) *with the steak. The Korean belief is the more banchan, the better luck you'll have, so pile it on.*

If you can't find gochugaru, the dried, smoky-sweet Korean red pepper powder, substitute gochujang, the sweetened paste version available at many well-stocked grocery stores (often called "Korean hot pepper paste"). The heat factor varies by brands, so start with a little and add more to taste.

―――――――― MAKES ABOUT 5 TO 6 SERVINGS ――――――――

Daikon Kimchee

1 pound daikon (about 1 large or 1 small bunch baby), peeled

1 teaspoon coarse sea or kosher salt

1½ tablespoons unseasoned rice vinegar

1 teaspoon Korean chile powder (gochugaru) or 1½ teaspoons Korean pepper paste (gochujang), more to taste

1½ tablespoons sugar (1 tablespoon if using sweetened chile paste)

1 medium clove garlic, minced

3 green onions, both white and tender green stems, sliced diagonally into ½-inch pieces

1½ teaspoons sesame seeds

Flank Steak

2 teaspoons whole black peppercorns, coarsely ground with a mortar and pestle

1 tablespoon whole coriander seeds, coarsely ground with a mortar and pestle

2 tablespoons soy sauce

2 tablespoons dark sesame oil

3 tablespoons vegetable oil

1. To make the kimchee, trim both ends off daikon and slice into 2-inch pieces. Make matchstick-like pieces by slicing each piece thinly lengthwise, stacking slices, and slicing again lengthwise. You should have about 4 cups.

2. In a medium bowl, toss daikon with salt and set aside for 20 minutes. Drain and rinse daikon well under cold running water, and roll in a kitchen towel to squeeze dry. Wipe out bowl and mix together rice vinegar, Korean chile powder or hot pepper paste, sugar (reduce to 1 tablespoon if using hot pepper paste), and garlic. Add drained daikon and toss to combine. Add more chile powder or paste to taste. Fold in green onions and sesame seeds. Cover and refrigerate for up to 1 week.

3. To the make steak marinade, combine peppercorns and coriander seeds, soy sauce, sesame oil, vegetable oil, sugar, jalapeño, garlic, and cilantro in a shallow pan large enough for steak to lay flat. Mix well, add steak, and coat both sides in marinade. Cover and refrigerate for 6 hours or overnight.

4. Thirty minutes before grilling, remove steak from refrigerator. Gently wipe off marinade with your hands into a small saucepan (leave any peppercorns and coriander clinging to meat) and place on a clean plate. Transfer marinade remaining in pan to saucepan and bring to a boil over medium-high heat. Reduce to a simmer and cook until marinade is slightly reduced, about 2 minutes,

stirring frequently to avoid burning. Set aside.

5. Heat a grill to medium high or place a stovetop grill pan over medium-high heat. When very hot, lightly pat steak with a paper towel. Sear for about 5 minutes per side for medium rare, 7 to 10 minutes per side for medium well, depending on thickness of steak. Remove from heat and brush with a tablespoon or two of reduced marinade. Loosely tent steak with foil and set aside to rest for 5 minutes. Thinly slice and serve immediately with kimchee and potato salad.

¼ cup sugar

½ medium jalapeño, roughly chopped, seeds removed for less heat if desired

1 medium clove garlic, minced

¼ medium bunch cilantro, both leaves and tender stems, roughly chopped

1½ pounds flank or skirt steak

To serve

German Potato Salad (*recipe page 80*)

MONKFISH SAUERBRATEN WITH PEARL ONIONS, NEW POTATOES & FAVAS

I admit that I've never really loved classic sauerbraten, the German equivalent of pot roast in a heavily spiced, vinegary marinade. It can get a little dry and heavy. I started making this monkfish version with red wine and balsamic vinegar at my first restaurant, years ago, and it's much more to my taste.

The brining process requires a little patience, but the marinade really intensifies the flavor of the mild fish. Ask your fishmonger to debone and remove the grayish membrane on the tail, the edible part of the fish.

MAKES 4 TO 5 SERVINGS

1. To make the marinade, in a medium sauté pan, cook bacon over medium-high heat until crispy. Transfer to paper towels to drain.

2. In the same pan, sauté carrot and celery root until just beginning to brown, 6 to 8 minutes. Stir in jam and scrape vegetables into a medium, nonreactive bowl or food storage container. Add wine, balsamic vinegar, thyme, bay leaf, salt, and peppercorns to vegetables. When completely cool, add monkfish to marinade (fish should be covered in marinade; if not, transfer to a smaller bowl). Cover with plastic wrap and refrigerate for 24 hours.

3. Preheat oven to 400°.

4. To make sauce, transfer monkfish to a plate and strain marinade into a medium saucepan. Discard vegetables and bacon. Add brown veal or chicken stock and balsamic vinegar, bring to a boil, and cook until reduced by more than half, about 15 minutes. Whisk in butter and season sauce with salt and pepper to taste.

5. Meanwhile, on a rimmed baking sheet, toss potatoes and onions with 2 tablespoons olive oil. Sprinkle generously with salt, and roast until golden brown and tender, stirring occasionally, about 16 to 20 minutes, depending on size of potatoes. Set aside.

(continued)

Marinade

1 slice thick, meaty bacon, roughly chopped

1 medium carrot, peeled and roughly chopped

½ small celery root, peeled and roughly chopped, or 1 large stalk celery, chopped

1 teaspoon raspberry jam

½ cup fruity red wine, such as Beaujolais

2½ tablespoons balsamic vinegar

1 sprig fresh thyme

1 bay leaf

½ teaspoon coarse sea or kosher salt

½ teaspoon whole black peppercorns

1¼ pounds whole, skinless monkfish fillet, backbone and membrane removed

Sauce & vegetables

1 cup Brown Veal Stock (*recipe page 194*) or Brown Chicken Stock (*recipe page 195*)

2 tablespoons balsamic vinegar

2 tablespoons unsalted butter, chilled

Coarse sea or kosher salt, to taste

Freshly ground pepper, to taste

1 pound assorted baby potatoes (1 to 2 inches), sliced in half if large

1 cup peeled pearl onions or spring onions, sliced in half if large

4 tablespoons extra-virgin olive oil, divided

½ cup fresh, shelled spring favas

6. In medium oven-proof sauté pan, heat remaining 2 tablespoons olive oil over medium-high heat. Pat monkfish dry with paper towels and sauté until golden brown on both sides, about 1½ minutes per side. Add ¼ cup of reduced marinade to pan, and transfer to oven. Bake until fish is just opaque in center, 10 to 15 minutes, depending on thickness of fillet. Remove from oven and allow to rest for 5 minutes before serving.

7. Meanwhile, in a medium saucepan, quickly blanch favas in 2 cups boiling water until crisp-tender, about 1 minute. Strain, rinse under cold water, and season with salt to taste. Add favas to baking sheet with potatoes. Just before serving, return vegetables to oven for 3 to 4 minutes to warm.

8. To serve, transfer whole fish to a serving plate and drizzle with remaining reduced marinade. Serve with roasted potatoes, onions, and favas.

LEMONY POTATOES

Himmel und erde are apples ("heaven") mashed with potatoes ("earth"). Apples are great, but I really love the brightness of California lemons. Rather than mash the two ingredients together, as in the traditional recipe, a quick boil adds a fresh, citrusy flavor. If mashed potatoes can ever taste like summer, this is it.

MAKES 4 TO 5 SERVINGS

1. Fill a medium pot halfway with water and bring to a low boil. Add potatoes, quartered lemons, and salt. Boil until potatoes are tender when pierced with a knife, 12 to 15 minutes. Strain.

2. Wipe out any remaining water in pot. Add milk and butter and gently heat until butter is melted, 1 to 2 minutes. Turn off heat.

3. Lightly squeeze lemons with tongs to extract some of the juice. Discard lemons and any seeds. Press warm potatoes through a ricer or food mill and add to pot. Stir to combine, and season to taste with salt and cayenne. Serve immediately.

2 pounds russet potatoes (about 5 to 6 medium), peeled and roughly chopped into 1-inch pieces

2 large lemons, quartered, and any surface seeds removed

1 teaspoon coarse sea or kosher salt, more to taste

1 cup whole milk

6 tablespoons (3 ounces) unsalted butter

Pinch cayenne pepper, or to taste

ROASTED ORZO "RISOTTO" WITH SUMMER VEGETABLES

Oven-roasting the orzo ahead of time makes quick work of a weeknight meal. Consider these vegetables a guideline, and vary them by the seasons.

MAKES 5 TO 6 SERVINGS

1 pound orzo pasta

5 tablespoons extra-virgin olive oil, divided

½ pound mixed mushrooms, such as oyster, crimini, and chanterelle, roughly chopped

½ teaspoon coarse sea or kosher salt, more to taste

1 medium shallot, diced

1 medium clove garlic, minced

2 sprigs thyme

¼ cup dry white wine

About 5 to 6 cups homemade Brown Chicken Stock (*recipe page 195*) or low-sodium chicken or vegetable broth, warmed

Kernels from 1 medium ear of corn

8 to 10 small brussels sprouts, leaves only

1 small or ½ large bunch asparagus, ends trimmed and sliced into 1-inch pieces

½ cup frozen peas, thawed and drained

3 tablespoons (1½ ounces) unsalted butter, divided

¾ cup grated parmesan, divided

Small handful pea tendrils

Freshly ground pepper, to taste

1. Preheat oven to 350° and place rack in middle of oven.

2. In a small bowl, toss orzo with 2 tablespoons olive oil and mix well to coat each grain. Spread pasta in single layer on a large rimmed baking sheet and toast in oven until dark golden brown, 18 to 22 minutes, stirring every 4 to 5 minutes to evenly brown. Watch closely the last 5 minutes to avoid burning. Allow pasta to cool completely and store for up to 2 days at room temperature.

3. In a medium Dutch oven or stockpot, heat 1 tablespoon olive oil over medium-high heat. Add mushrooms and sauté until beginning to brown, 6 to 8 minutes. Season with salt to taste and transfer to a plate.

4. In same pot, heat remaining 2 tablespoons olive oil over medium-high heat. Add shallot and garlic and sauté until just tender, 1 to 2 minutes. Add orzo and thyme, cook 1 minute, stirring constantly, and then deglaze with wine. When wine evaporates, add 2 cups vegetable stock and ½ teaspoon salt. Cook until liquid is almost evaporated, stirring frequently. Add corn, brussels sprouts leaves, asparagus, and 1 cup stock. Continue to cook pasta, stirring frequently and adding 1 additional cup of stock whenever liquid is almost evaporated, until al dente, 24 to 28 minutes.

5. Add thawed peas, reduce heat to low, and gradually stir in butter, 1 tablespoon at a time, then ½ cup parmesan. Remove thyme sprigs, add pea tendrils, and season with salt and pepper to taste. If pasta seems dry, add a little more stock. Divide risotto among serving bowls, and sprinkle with remaining ¼ cup parmesan. Serve immediately.

DAS FEST

TIME FOR A FEAST

So many of our American holiday customs are rooted in Germanic traditions: Oktoberfest, certainly, but also Mardi Gras, an evolution of *Fastnacht* (the night of celebrating before the Lenten fast). Even the Easter bunny has Teutonic roots—in the 1700s, early Pennsylvania Dutch settlers brought the *osterhase*, or egg-laying hare, legend with them across the Atlantic.

Hands down my favorite time of year is the *Weihnachten* (Christmas) season. No one does Christmas like the Germans! There's nothing quite like enjoying the holidays in the place where so many of our Christmas traditions began. In Germany, when fir trees were first brought indoors, they were decorated with candies, pastries, and later, hand-blown glass ornaments from Lauscha, a central mountain town still renowned for its glass artisans. If you ever have an opportunity to visit Germany in December, don't pass it up.

Our restaurants in Los Angeles are also busiest during the winter holidays, when we serve seasonal specialties like roast goose with red cabbage. Across town, the bakery never sleeps, turning out thousands of holiday breads, cakes, and cookies by hand each day. It's true that the holidays that can be a little overwhelming. But as soon as the first *lebkuchen* (the original gingerbread) comes out of the oven, it smells like home, and I'm happy and ready to celebrate.

RABBIT RILLETTES WITH GRAPPA

When I opened my first restaurant, game meats were a tough menu sell and even harder to find. That was a shame, as the country-style pâtés that you find all over Europe are especially good when made with lean, delicately flavored game meats like rabbit. They're incredible easy to make, portable, and do triple duty when slathered on fresh bread as an appetizer or light lunch or supper.

Today, I'm happy to say that you can find sustainable, farm-raised rabbit at many farmers' markets and butcher shops, and rillettes and pâtés are common on the menus at the more adventurous American restaurants.

MAKES ABOUT 2 CUPS

1. Combine wine, chicken stock, grappa or pisco, garlic, bay leaf, thyme, coriander, salt, and pepper in a medium bowl. Submerge rabbit in brine, cover, and refrigerate overnight or for up to 24 hours.

2. Transfer rabbit and brine to a large Dutch oven and place over high heat. Bring to a boil, reduce heat to a simmer, and skim any foam that rises to top. Partially cover pot with lid and cook until meat is fall-apart tender, about 3 hours, flipping rabbit pieces once if necessary for even cooking.

3. Remove rabbit from broth and set aside on a plate until cool enough to handle, about 30 minutes. With your hands, finely shred meat, discarding bones and skin. In a medium bowl, lightly whip 6 tablespoons butter with a rubber spatula or spoon until no lumps remain. Add meat and fold together until well incorporated. Mixture should look slightly creamy; if dry, add additional 2 tablespoons butter. Season with salt and pepper to taste.

4. Tightly pack meat into a medium crock or two 8-ounce ramekins. Sprinkle with fresh thyme leaves, cover, and refrigerate overnight. Allow to sit at room temperature at least 1 hour before serving with Melba toast or toasted bread. Refrigerate for up to 1 week; press plastic wrap onto surface of meat before storing.

1 cup dry white wine

3 cups low-sodium chicken stock, preferably homemade (*recipe page 195*)

½ cup grappa or pisco

2 medium cloves garlic, minced

1 bay leaf

1 teaspoon fresh thyme leaves, more for garnish

1 teaspoon whole coriander seeds

1 teaspoon coarse sea or kosher salt, more to taste

1 teaspoon freshly ground pepper, more to taste

1 whole rabbit, about 2 to 2½ pounds, cut into 4 or 5 pieces, giblets reserved for another use

6 to 8 tablespoons (3 to 4 ounces) unsalted butter, room temperature

Melba toast or toasted bread like Sourdough Roggen Brot (*recipe page 22*), for serving

PEPPER-CRUSTED SHORT RIBS WITH BRUSSELS SPROUTS GIARDINIERA & HORSERADISH

As with any good steak, curing short ribs in the refrigerator slightly dries out the surface of the meat so you get a really flavorful, dark brown crust. Resist the urge to cover the ribs even loosely with plastic wrap. You're basically creating a temporary aging room inside your fridge. I like the crunchy contrast of the pickled vegetables with the meat, but your favorite potatoes and a few mustards (see page 196) are also good.

The English-cut short ribs you can get from a good butcher are much meatier than the "flanken" style found at most grocery stores. Save those for goulash (see page 129).

_____ MAKES ABOUT 6 SERVINGS _____

4 bone-in English-cut beef short ribs (4½ to 5 pounds total)

Brine

⅓ cup kosher salt

1 tablespoon honey

½ large lemon, sliced ¼ inch thick and seeds removed

1 sprig thyme

2 medium cloves garlic, thinly sliced

1 bay leaf

1 teaspoon black peppercorns

Cure

⅔ cup whole rainbow peppercorn mix

2 tablespoons whole coriander seeds

Roasting & serving

¼ cup dry white wine

Brussels Sprouts Giardiniera (*recipe page 145*), for serving

Good-quality horseradish, for serving

1. Two days before you plan to serve the short ribs, prepare the brine. Bring 1 cup water, salt, honey, lemon, thyme, garlic, bay leaf, and black peppercorns to a boil in a small saucepan. Remove from heat and allow to steep for 10 minutes. Combine brine with 3 cups ice-cold water.

2. Snugly fit short ribs in a single layer in a large glass or ceramic baking dish or 2 smaller loaf pans. When brine is completely cool, pour over ribs (they should be completely covered). Discard any leftover brine. Cover and refrigerate for 18 to 24 hours.

3. To make the cure, toast the rainbow peppercorns and coriander in large sauté pan over medium-high heat until fragrant, about 1 minute. In a spice or coffee grinder, roughly grind peppercorn mixture until coarse. Transfer to a large platter.

4. Discard the brine and rinse ribs under cold running water. Shake off excess water and roll in pepper mix, pressing spices firmly into all sides to make a crust (bone-side can be less thickly covered). Place ribs on a small baking rack. Set rack on a rimmed sheet pan or over a small pan to catch any drippings and refrigerate, uncovered, for another 18 to 24 hours.

5. To roast short ribs, preheat oven to 350° and place rack in middle of oven.

6. Place ribs in a single layer, bone-side down, in large roasting pan or heavy-bottomed saucepan. Tent with aluminum foil and tuck foil around meat to loosely cover. Roast for 1 hour, 15 minutes, remove pan from oven, and add white wine. Turn each rib on its side gently (try not to remove too much of crust), tent again with foil, and roast for 1 more hour. Flip ribs again to opposite side, tent, and continue to roast until ribs are tender but still hold together when pierced with a fork, about 45 minutes to 1 hour, 15 minutes or longer. Total roasting time is 3 to 3½ hours. Remove ribs from oven and allow to rest for 10 minutes.

7. Remove bones and slice each rib into 4 or 5 slices. Arrange bones on a serving platter with sliced meat arranged as if it were still attached to the bone. Serve immediately with giardiniera and horseradish.

BRUSSELS SPROUTS GIARDINIERA

One of the many reasons I like to keep some giardiniera in the fridge is so I can add it to whatever vegetable looks good at the farmers' market. In winter, it's often brussels sprouts.

MAKES ABOUT 4 CUPS

1. Remove the brussels sprouts leaves one by one and place in a medium bowl. Stop when you get to the smallest leaves around the core (discard the core).

2. Fill a medium saucepan halfway with water and bring to a boil. Add salt and brussels sprouts leaves, reduce to a simmer, and blanch until bright green and tender, about 1 minute. Drain and immediately rinse under cold water. Lightly squeeze sprouts dry in a kitchen towel.

3. In a large bowl, mix together blanched brussels sprouts, giardiniera, celery, and juice of ¼ lemon. Season with additional lemon juice, salt, and pepper to taste. Serve immediately, or refrigerate up to 2 days. Bring to room temperature before serving.

½ pound (about 8 to 10) large brussels sprouts

½ teaspoon coarse sea or kosher salt, more to taste

3 cups Giardiniera (recipe page 201), room temperature

1 medium stalk celery, sliced in ¼-inch half-moons

¼ medium lemon, more to taste

Freshly ground pepper, to taste

ROAST GOOSE WITH CITRUS-SPICED RED CABBAGE

I've never gotten used to seeing turkey on holiday tables instead of weihnachtsgans *(Christmas goose). Goose is all moist, dark meat, so you never have the problem of a dry bird.*

To ensure a crispy skin, dry the goose well, inside and out, and refrigerate the bird for two full days—uncovered. As with the short ribs (see page 142), *you're creating a mock aging room that helps develop a richer flavor. And don't throw away all that good fat—use it to make the best roasted potatoes you've ever tasted.*

SERVES ABOUT 8

1 (12- to 14-pound) whole goose, fully thawed

Kosher salt and freshly ground pepper, to taste

Citrus-Spiced Red Cabbage (*recipe page 78*)

Goose Fat Potatoes

Slice baby fingerling or other small potatoes in half and toss generously with goose fat. Place on a rimmed baking sheet and roast at 350° until potatoes are caramelized and tender, stirring once or twice for even coloring, about 30 to 40 minutes (depending on size of potatoes). Sprinkle generously with sea salt and freshly ground pepper.

1. Two days before you plan to roast the goose, remove the giblets and neck and save for another use. With your hands, pull off the soft fat in the bird's cavity and around the neck. Save fat for rendering (recipe below). Pat exterior and cavity of goose dry with paper towels and refrigerate, uncovered, for 36 to 48 hours.

2. Preheat oven to 325° and place rack in middle of oven. Remove goose from refrigerator 2 hours before roasting.

3. Pat goose dry again with paper towels and generously sprinkle all over with salt and pepper. Place on a rack in a deep roasting pan and roast for 2 hours, basting occasionally with fat in pan. Carefully remove from oven and use a ladle to scoop out excess fat (as much as 2 cups). Reserve fat for another use.

4. Return goose to oven, lower the temperature to 300°, and continue to roast, basting occasionally with fat that accumulates in pan, until flesh is tender when pierced and a meat thermometer inserted into breast registers 165°, about 1½ to 2 hours longer. Remove goose from oven and set aside to rest for 20 to 30 minutes before carving. Serve with Citrus-Spiced Red Cabbage.

How to Render Goose Fat

In a medium saucepan, bring trimmed fat and 2 tablespoons of water to a simmer. Reduce heat to low, and slowly cook until fat has rendered (water will evaporate) and only small pieces of fat remain, about 30 minutes. Strain through a fine-mesh strainer and cool to room temperature. Refrigerate for up to 1 month or freeze.

GRILLED STEAKS WITH CAFÉ DE PARIS BUTTER & HERB SPÄTZLE

Café de Paris butter became popular in the 1940s at a Geneva restaurant by the same name. Those flavored compound butters of the 1980s could never measure up. It's fantastic on any cut of steak, which is how it was originally served at the restaurant. But the butter makes almost everything it touches taste better, from potatoes and steamed vegetables to chicken and pork. Make a big batch and freeze the butter in small portions.

Other than the reduced veal stock, most of the ingredients in this recipe are pantry staples. Keep this recipe in the back of your mind when you have a bumper crop of herbs in your produce drawer.

—————— MAKES ABOUT 1¼ POUNDS BUTTER ——————

Butter

1 tablespoon fresh thyme leaves, chopped

1 tablespoon fresh marjoram or oregano leaves, chopped

1 tablespoon fresh rosemary, finely chopped

1 tablespoon chives, finely chopped

1 tablespoon parsley leaves, finely chopped

10 tarragon leaves, finely chopped

2 tablespoons minced shallots

1 medium clove garlic, minced

2 tablespoon capers, drained, rinsed, and finely chopped

4 small anchovy fillets, rinsed and finely chopped

½ teaspoon curry powder

½ teaspoon sweet paprika

½ teaspoon cayenne pepper

1 tablespoon coarse sea or kosher salt

1½ tablespoons freshly ground pepper

1 tablespoon cognac

1½ teaspoons Worcestershire

2 tablespoons ketchup

2 tablespoons Dijon mustard

¼ cup heavy cream

2 tablespoons warm Glace de Viande (reduced veal stock), store-bought or homemade (*recipe page 195*)

1 pound unsalted butter, at warm room temperature but not melted

To serve

Tenderloin or your favorite cut of steak, grilled as you prefer

Spätzle (*recipe page 123*) with mixed fresh herbs

1. In a stand mixer fitted with the paddle attachment, mix together all ingredients except butter on low speed. Add softened butter and continue to mix until well combined and no white flecks of butter remain, about 30 seconds. Alternatively, mix ingredients together by hand in a medium bowl with a rubber spatula or wooden spoon. Turn out butter onto a large plastic cutting board, place a piece of plastic wrap on top, and mash butter with the heel of your hand to fully incorporate.

2. Turn out ¼ of butter onto a 10- to 12-inch sheet of plastic wrap and form into a log (butter will be very soft, the log doesn't need to be perfectly shaped). Roughly seal plastic wrap in center of log and twist to tighten both ends like a sausage casing. Repeat with remaining butter so you have 4 logs. Refrigerate butter until firm, about 2 hours.

3. To serve, while still warm, top each grilled steak with 1 generous slice of butter. Serve immediately with spätzle.

4. Refrigerate remaining butter for up to 1 week, or freeze in freezer bags for up to 3 months. Thaw frozen butter for 15 minutes and slice off small portions as needed.

GINGERED CARROTS

This make-ahead side gets a double hit of ginger, both fresh and pickled. To make a vegan version, use vegetable stock and omit the cream. Mirin and pickled ginger are available at well-stocked grocery stores and Asian markets.

MAKES ABOUT 5 TO 6 SERVINGS

1. In a large saucepan, heat butter over medium heat. When butter begins to bubble and foam subsides, add shallot and sauté until translucent, about 2 minutes. Add garlic and sauté for 30 seconds. Add mirin, ginger, carrots, and enough vegetable or chicken stock to just cover vegetables. Bring to a boil, reduce heat, and simmer until carrots are crisp-tender, 18 to 22 minutes.

2. Strain carrots over a medium bowl, reserving stock. Return carrots to pan and add hot sauce, pickled ginger and juice, cream, and ½ cup of cooking stock. Stir to combine and add additional cooking stock and salt to taste. Serve immediately.

3. If making ahead, cool completely and refrigerate for up to 3 days. Gently re-warm in a large saucepan over medium heat.

1 tablespoon unsalted butter

¼ large shallot, minced (about 1½ tablespoons)

½ medium clove garlic, minced

2 tablespoons mirin (sweet Japanese rice wine)

1 tablespoon finely grated fresh ginger

4 cups peeled and grated carrots (about 1¼ pounds)

2½ to 3 cups homemade or low-sodium vegetable or chicken stock, as needed (*recipe page 195*)

Dash of hot sauce, such as Tabasco

2 tablespoons pickled ginger, coarsely chopped

1½ teaspoons pickled ginger juice (from pickled ginger jar)

3 tablespoons heavy cream

Kosher salt, to taste

ROASTED ROOT VEGETABLE SALAD WITH LEMON & THYME MAYONNAISE

Root vegetables like kohlrabi and parsnips have a subtle earthiness that adds a unique taste to a roasted vegetable salad. The harmony here comes from the simplicity of the contrasting ingredients: the slight anise flavor of fennel, the sweetness of the beets. You can even add radishes to the mix.

Roasting the vegetables separately is a little more time consuming, but it's key so they all get the right crisp-tender consistency. You can roast them all ahead. If you're using red beets, make sure to dress them separately to avoid staining the other vegetables with beet juice.

MAKES 6 TO 8 SERVINGS

Roasted Vegetables

6 tablespoons extra-virgin olive oil, divided

1 medium kohlrabi, peeled, sliced ¼-inch thick, and roughly chopped into 1-inch pieces

2 bunches baby carrots, unpeeled and sliced in half lengthwise, or quartered if thick

2 medium fennel bulbs, halved lengthwise and sliced into ¼-inch-thick half moons

Coarse sea or kosher salt, to taste

2 medium sweet potatoes, peeled, sliced ¼-inch thick, and roughly chopped into 1-inch pieces

1 bunch baby beets, tops removed, peeled and sliced in half if large

1 tablespoon water

Thyme Mayonnaise

1 large egg yolk

2 tablespoons white wine vinegar

1 small clove garlic, roughly chopped

½ teaspoon coarse sea or kosher salt

½ cup extra-virgin olive oil

1 tablespoon fresh thyme leaves

1. To make roasted vegetables, preheat oven to 350° and place both racks in middle of oven.

2. Place kohlrabi, carrots, and fennel on 3 small baking sheets or in 3 baking dishes. Toss each with 1 tablespoon olive oil, sprinkle with salt, and scatter vegetables in a single layer. Place each in oven and roast until all are crisp-tender, about 18 to 22 minutes for fennel and 25 to 35 minutes for kohlrabi and carrots, depending on size. Stir once or twice throughout cooking for even browning. Remove from oven and transfer all to a large bowl.

3. Meanwhile, toss sweet potatoes with 2 tablespoons olive oil and sprinkle with salt. Scatter on a baking sheet or baking dish, loosely tent with foil, and roast for 15 minutes. Uncover, stir, and continue to roast until potatoes are very tender, about 15 to 20 minutes longer. Transfer to same bowl as kohlrabi, carrots, and fennel. When cool, cover and refrigerate for up to 3 days.

4. Toss beets with remaining 1 tablespoon olive oil and water and sprinkle with salt. Cover tightly with foil and roast until fork-tender, anywhere from 25 to 40 minutes (baby beets vary greatly in size). Allow to cool and set aside. When cool, cover and refrigerate for up to 3 days.

5. To make the mayonnaise, in a blender combine egg yolk, vinegar, garlic, and salt, and mix on low until well combined. With blender running, very slowly add olive oil until dressing is emulsified. Add thyme leaves and pulse just to combine. Cover and refrigerate for up to 3 days.

6. To assemble the salad, allow vegetables to come to room temperature. Toss with lemon juice (if beets are red, dress separately with 1 teaspoon lemon juice) and all but 1 tablespoon of chives. Season with salt, pepper, and additional lemon juice to taste. Arrange vegetables on a serving platter and top with beets and goat cheese. Drizzle half of thyme mayonnaise on top, and sprinkle with remaining tablespoon of chives. Serve additional thyme mayonnaise on the side.

To serve

2 tablespoons freshly squeezed lemon juice, more to taste

1 small bunch chives, roughly chopped, divided

4 ounces goat cheese, crumbled

Coarse sea or kosher salt, to taste

Freshly ground pepper, to taste

ROASTED CAULIFLOWER WITH POMEGRANATE, RAISINS & HAZELNUTS

With so many flavors on the holiday table, I gravitate toward lightly dressed vegetable sides with hints of spice.

MAKES 8 TO 10 SERVINGS AS A SIDE DISH

1. In a small bowl, combine raisins and orange juice. Cover and soak at room temperature overnight.

2. Preheat oven to 400°.

3. In a medium jar, combine 3 tablespoons olive oil, vinegar, cinnamon, allspice, ¼ teaspoon salt, pepper, honey, and lime juice. Shake well and set dressing aside.

4. Divide cauliflower into medium florets. You should have 8 to 10 generous cups. Place on a large rimmed baking sheet and toss with remaining 2 tablespoons oil and ½ teaspoon salt. Roast until florets are tender when pierced, stirring occasionally to evenly brown, 20 to 25 minutes. Remove from oven and transfer to a large bowl.

5. Strain raisins and discard juice. Add raisins to cauliflower with hazelnuts, pomegranate seeds, parsley leaves, and about ¾ of dressing. Toss well and season with salt, pepper, and additional dressing to taste. Serve immediately or at room temperature.

½ cup golden raisins

Juice of 1 medium orange

5 tablespoons extra-virgin olive oil, divided

1½ tablespoons Champagne or white wine vinegar

⅛ teaspoon ground cinnamon

⅛ teaspoon ground allspice

¾ teaspoon coarse sea or kosher salt, divided, more to taste

½ teaspoon freshly ground pepper, more to taste

1 tablespoon honey, warmed for 5 seconds in the microwave or on the stovetop

1 tablespoon freshly squeezed lime juice

1 large or about 2 to 3 small heads cauliflower (2½ to 3 pounds total)

1 cup blanched hazelnuts, lightly toasted and roughly chopped (*see page 193*)

3 tablespoons pomegranate seeds

¼ cup parsley leaves, torn in half if large

POTATO-ALMOND CROQUETTES

Breading and frying leftover potatoes is always good, whether you call them croquettes, potato cakes, or sure, tater tots. Instead of leftovers, I prefer to start with freshly boiled potatoes and draw out some of the excess moisture. Make the potato base ahead and fry the croquettes just before serving, or re-warm them in the oven for a dinner party.

The almonds will burn if the oil gets too hot, so regulate the temperature closely.

MAKES 16 CROQUETTES, ABOUT 8 SERVINGS

1½ pounds russet potatoes, peeled and roughly chopped into 1-inch pieces

1½ teaspoons coarse sea or kosher salt, divided, more to taste

3 large whole eggs, lightly beaten, plus 2 large egg yolks, divided

Two generous pinches nutmeg

4 tablespoons (2 ounces) unsalted butter, melted

¾ cup flour, more if needed

2 cups thinly sliced, blanched almonds

Freshly ground pepper

Small handful parsley leaves, finely chopped

1. Fill a medium stockpot halfway with water and bring to a boil. Add potatoes and 1 teaspoon salt, reduce to a simmer, and cook until potatoes are very tender, 18 to 22 minutes. Strain and toss potatoes in strainer to remove excess water. Immediately spread potatoes in a single layer on a rimmed baking sheet. Set aside, uncovered, until potatoes begin to dry out and turn white around edges, 20 to 30 minutes.

2. Over a large bowl, press potatoes through a food mill or ricer. Stir in 2 egg yolks, remaining ½ teaspoon salt, and nutmeg. Add melted butter, mix well, and chill for at least 1 hour.

3. Divide potatoes into 16 pieces about the size of golf balls. Shape each into roughly 4" x 1" logs approximately 1 inch tall. They do not need to be perfectly shaped. Cover and refrigerate overnight.

4. Place flour in one small bowl and remaining 3 whole beaten eggs in another bowl. Place almonds on a plate and lightly crush with your hands so large chunks remain.

5. Roll each potato log in flour, then egg, shaking off any excess egg. Roll in almonds, pressing sides gently to adhere. Refrigerate croquettes while you prepare fryer.

6. Line a baking sheet with 2 to 3 layers of paper towels. If serving immediately, preheat oven to 250°. Fill a small, deep saucepan with 2 to 3 inches of oil, and use a thermometer to monitor the temperature. If using a deep fryer, set temperature to 325°.

7. When oil reaches 325°, use a slotted spoon to gently transfer 3 to 4 croquettes to saucepan, depending on size of pan, and fry until light golden brown, about 2½ to 3 minutes. (If using a deep fryer, you may be able to fry more at one time.) Use a slotted spoon or the fry basket to transfer croquettes to paper towels. Immediately sprinkle generously with salt. If serving immediately, transfer to oven to keep warm. Repeat with remaining croquettes, sprinkle with parsley, and serve.

8. If making ahead, store croquettes at room temperature on a baking sheet lined with a wire rack for up to 2 hours. When cool, loosely tent with foil. To re-warm, transfer tented croquettes to oven and bake at 350° until warm, about 5 minutes.

HOLIDAY BAKING

When I was growing up, other than making just a few kinds of cookies at home, families bought most of their holiday sweets. The pastries sold at local bakeshops, many of which were helmed by a long line of master bakers, were just so much better than what anyone thought they could make at home. During the winter, you could almost follow the aroma of cinnamon, cloves, and anise straight to the shops filled with stacks of lebkuchen and stollen.

When I moved to the States, I discovered that "lucking into leckerli," a honey and spice bar cookie, wasn't as easy. If I wanted quality traditional sweets, I had to make them myself—so I did. Today, we have an entire bakery menu dedicated to the traditional German holiday breads and cookies that I was raised on.

GLÜHWEIN

What's not to love about a holiday tradition that doubles as fuel for weekend baking projects? Even in Los Angeles, winter nights are cool enough to justify a pot of mulled wine on the stove.

——— MAKES 4 TO 8 SERVINGS, DEPENDING ON HOW *WEIN*-FRIENDLY THE CROWD IS ———

1. In a medium stockpot, combine wine, cinnamon stick, star anise, and sugar.

2. Spike orange all over with cloves. Slice in half, being careful not to cut cloves, and add to pot. Bring to a boil, reduce heat, and simmer for 10 minutes. Remove glühwein from heat and set aside to cool for 10 minutes.

3. Remove orange and spices and discard. Serve glühwein immediately, or cool completely and refrigerate for up to 3 days. Re-warm over low heat (do not boil) before serving.

2 bottles fruity red wine, such as Beaujolais

1 cinnamon stick

3 whole star anise

1 cup sugar

1 medium orange

8 whole cloves

SPEKULATIUS

Spekulatius are thin, crunchy, lightly sweetened cut-out cookies— the precursor to animal crackers. My most recent (and completely irrational) purchase was a huge antique machine to stamp out the cookies. I tend to get a little excited about these kinds of things.

My friend Ralf, a master baker from Germany, shipped the massive metal cut-outs over piece by piece and painstakingly reassembled the press at our bakery ("danke" is an understatement). He then trained us in the art of making the most delicious almond-speckled crackers. They're not too sweet, and they're the perfect accompaniment to tea or glühwein.

───────── MAKES 3 TO 4 DOZEN COOKIES, DEPENDING ON SIZE OF CUTTERS ─────────

½ cup (4 ounces) unsalted butter, room temperature

1 tablespoon honey

⅓ cup plus 1 tablespoon sugar

⅓ cup packed brown sugar

2 large eggs yolks, divided

¼ teaspoon kosher salt

⅓ cup plus 1 tablespoon whole milk, divided

2 cups flour, more for rolling out cookies

½ cup plus 1 tablespoon finely ground almonds, also known as almond flour

1 teaspoon cinnamon

Generous ¼ teaspoon ground cloves

Generous ¼ teaspoon ground coriander

Generous ¼ teaspoon ground anise seed (*see page 191*)

1½ teaspoons baking powder

1 cup thinly sliced (not slivered) almonds, divided

1. In a stand mixer fitted with the paddle attachment, combine softened butter, honey, sugar, and brown sugar. Mix on medium speed briefly, add 1 egg yolk and salt, and mix until well incorporated, about 30 seconds. Add ⅓ cup milk, cover with a kitchen towel (to avoid splashing), and mix well until creamy, about 1 minute.

2. In a medium bowl, whisk together flour, finely ground almonds, cinnamon, cloves, coriander, anise seed, and baking powder. Add dry ingredients to stand mixer and mix on low speed until dough comes together and begins to stick to the paddle, about 1 minute. Divide dough in half, flatten into 5-inch discs, and cover with plastic wrap. Refrigerate at least 2 hours or overnight.

3. Preheat oven to 350° and place racks in top and bottom third of oven. Place dough on a work surface and lightly knead by pressing and folding the dough with the palm of your hand about 8 to 10 times. If dough has been refrigerated overnight, knead a few more times. Sprinkle the work surface generously with flour and sprinkle about half of the almonds on top of the flour. Place dough round in the middle of almonds and roll ¼-inch thick (if using cookie cutters, size of rectangle doesn't matter; if using a spekulatius roller, make about an 8" x 12" rectangle to make two rows, depending on width of cutter). Dust dough with additional flour if needed. Gently lift dough and redistribute almonds to any areas lacking nuts.

4. Use 2- to 3-inch cookie cutters to cut out spekulatius and transfer to an unlined baking sheet. If using a spekulatius roller, sprinkle top of dough lightly with flour and press down firmly to cut through dough when rolling. (If dough begins to stick to roller, peel off and re-flour). Pull apart roller cookies or use a knife to cut them out further, if needed.

5. In a small bowl, lightly beat together remaining egg yolk and remaining 1 tablespoon milk. Use a pastry brush or your fingers to lightly brush cookies with egg wash. Bake until cookies begin to turn light brown around the edges and on the bottom, about 14 to 16 minutes, rotating pans front to back and top to bottom halfway through. Allow cookies to rest for 1 to 2 minutes and immediately transfer with spatula to a rack. Cool completely and store tightly covered at room temperature for up to 5 days.

LECKERLI

Leckerli are descendants of fifteenth-century honey-sweetened citrus cookies flavored by the spice trade. At the bakery, we use heavy-duty stand mixers to mix the very stiff dough. At home, I use a little muscle and do it the old-fashioned way, kneading the eggs into the dough with my hands.

Baker's ammonia results in a pleasantly chewier texture, but baking powder also works well. As for the candied lemon and orange peels, look for them in specialty markets or online.

MAKES ABOUT 40 BAR COOKIES

6 cups flour

1 teaspoon baker's ammonia (*see page 163*) dissolved in 2 teaspoons water, or 2 teaspoons baking powder

½ teaspoon kosher salt

2 tablespoons cinnamon

1½ teaspoons ground cloves

1 teaspoon ground anise seed (*see page 191*)

1 teaspoon ground coriander

2 cups slivered (not sliced) almonds or roughly chopped whole, blanched almonds

1 teaspoon lemon zest

1 teaspoon orange zest

⅔ cup finely chopped candied lemon peel

⅔ cup finely chopped candied orange peel

2¼ cups honey

1 cup sugar

4 large egg yolks, lightly beaten

Topping

2 cups confectioner's sugar

1 cup slivered almonds or roughly chopped whole, blanched almonds, lightly toasted (*see page 193*)

1. Preheat oven to 375° and place rack in middle of oven. Butter a 9" x 13" baking dish, preferably a metal quarter-sheet pan with a 1-inch rim. A metal or glass baking dish with higher sides can be substituted. Line dish with a single sheet of parchment paper, lengthwise, that extends about 1½ inches up both ends.

2. In a large bowl, mix together flour, baker's ammonia or baking powder, salt, cinnamon, cloves, anise seed, and coriander. Add almonds, lemon and orange zests, and candied lemon and orange peels, and mix well.

3. In a medium saucepan, combine honey and sugar. Heat over medium-high heat until sugar dissolves, 3 to 4 minutes, stirring often. Pour half of honey over flour mixture and use a large spoon to mix together. Add remaining honey and continue to stir; flour will not be fully incorporated.

4. Turn out dough onto large work surface. Make a slight depression in the center of the dough and place egg yolks in center. Gradually work eggs into dough, pressing dough with the palms of your hands as if kneading stiff bread dough. When eggs and flour are fully incorporated, transfer to parchment-lined pan and use your palms to flatten as evenly as possible in the pan, pressing down firmly.

5. Bake until edges are beginning to brown and center is only slightly glossy, 18 to 20 minutes, rotating pan front to back through. Transfer to a rack and cool for 5 minutes. Run a knife around edges and use parchment overhang to slide cookies onto a large cutting board or flat work surface while warm.

6. Meanwhile, make topping. In a small bowl, whisk together confectioner's sugar and ¼ cup lukewarm water until the consistency of molasses. If too thick to spread, add another splash of water. Use an offset spatula or blunt knife to spread glaze over warm cookies immediately after removing from baking pan. Sprinkle with toasted almonds and press down lightly to adhere. When cool, cut into thin, 1" x 3" rectangles.

Baker's Ammonia

Baker's ammonia, also known as ammonia carbonate, is a traditional leavening agent. In the Middle Ages, it was made from deer antlers and known as *hartshorn* ("hart" is an old word for male stag). The commercial version today is manufactured synthetically.

Baker's ammonia, which can have a strong flavor, has been replaced almost entirely by such leavening agents as baking powder and baking soda, but I still like to bake with it. When used in traditional cookies like lebkuchen and leckerli, the large surface area helps the ammonia escape, and in return, the cookies develop more air pockets and a subtle, almost chewy crunch.

Baker's ammonia is available at specialty pastry shops and online, including from King Arthur Flour. Dissolve 1 teaspoon in 2 teaspoons of water before adding to a recipe. Or substitute twice as much baking powder for baker's ammonia (do not dissolve in water). Note: Do not use household ammonia, an entirely different and poisonous product.

VANILLEKIPFERL

Also known as Viennese crescent cookies, vanillekipferl *are similar to sand tarts, only with ground almonds or hazelnuts in the dough. They're fun for even the tiniest fingers to shape and dust in powdered sugar.*

Vanilla-bean paste gives the cookies an authentic speckled charm, but you can substitute good-quality vanilla extract.

————————— MAKES ABOUT 40 SMALL COOKIES —————————

1 cup finely ground almonds, also known as almond flour

2½ cups flour

½ teaspoon kosher salt

1 cup (8 ounces) unsalted butter, at room temperature, more as needed

⅔ cup plus 1 tablespoon sugar, plus ½ cup sugar for topping cookies

1 tablespoon light corn syrup

2 large egg yolks

2¼ teaspoons vanilla bean paste or vanilla extract, divided

1. In a large bowl, whisk together ground almonds, flour, and salt.

2. In a stand mixer fitted with the paddle attachment, cream butter, ⅔ cup plus 1 tablespoon sugar, and corn syrup on medium speed until well combined, about 1 minute. Add egg yolks and 2 teaspoons vanilla bean paste or extract and mix well again, scraping down paddle and bowl. Add half of flour mixture and mix on low speed until incorporated, about 30 seconds. Add remaining flour and mix just until a rough dough forms. Remove bowl from stand mixer and press dough together with your hands; it will be very crumbly. If necessary, lightly butter your hands to help dough hold together.

3. Divide dough in half. Cover each half in plastic wrap and shape into two 5-inch discs. Refrigerate for 1 hour.

4. Preheat oven to 325° and place racks in top and bottom third of oven.

5. Remove one round of dough from refrigerator. Roll roughly tablespoon-size pieces into small logs about 3 inches long. Shape log into a crescent and place cookies 1½ inches apart on one or two ungreased baking sheets.

6. Bake until bottoms of cookies are very lightly golden brown on bottom (tops will not color), about 16 to 18 minutes, rotating pans top to bottom and front to back halfway through. To check, lift the edge of one cookie (consider it baker's luck if the cookie breaks). Remove cookies from oven and cool for 5 minutes on baking sheet.

7. In a small bowl, combine remaining ¼ teaspoon vanilla bean paste or extract and ½ cup sugar. Mix with your fingers until well combined.

8. While still warm, use a spatula to loosen cookies from baking sheet. Transfer 2 to 3 at a time to vanilla-sugar bowl and gently roll in sugar to evenly coat. Set aside on a rack to cool completely and repeat with remaining dough. Store up to 1 week in a sealed container.

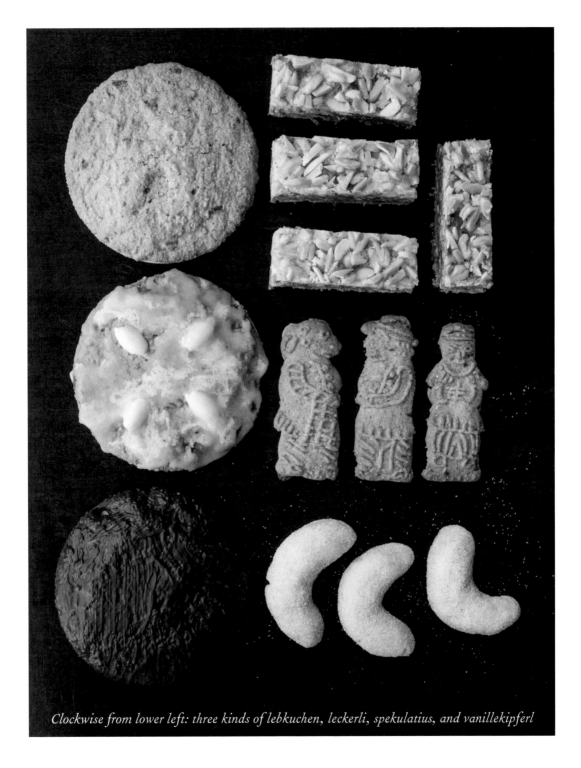

Clockwise from lower left: three kinds of lebkuchen, leckerli, spekulatius, and vanillekipferl

GINGERBREAD ANCESTRY

Gingerbread unofficially arrived on the baking scene when medieval monks tossed new spice-merchant finds like cinnamon, cloves, anise, ginger, and cardamom into their honey cakes. Every baker, then as well as today, had his own "secret" spice mixture. These spice cakes spread to convents and, later, to bakers throughout Europe. The dough was eventually transformed into more modern cookie forms, often seen in different cut-out shapes.

During the holiday season these days, you'll find good-luck pigs, gingerbread houses, and yes, plenty of gingerbread people among the countless versions in German and Austrian bakeries. My favorite is still the classic round elisen lebkuchen of Nuremberg, made with traditional ingredients and still baked on top of thin, communion wafer–like biscuits called *oblaten*. In this country, the word "gingerbread" evolved to mean holiday cookies that literally have ginger in them. Though my lebkuchen don't have ginger, I still consider them "gingerbread," as they have that spice-cake flavor that is so essential during the holiday season.

ELISEN LEBKUCHEN

For years, I wasn't satisfied with the flavor and texture of my recipe for lebkuchen, a cake-like spice cookie, but now I think I've finally got it. Any cookie once protected by guilds, meaning it was illegal to make them other than by certified experts, deserves the honor of obsessive recipe testing. The cookies keep for a long time and taste better as they age, so you can check them off your holiday baking list early.

Look for oblaten wafers at specialty baking shops and European delis, or you can order them online.

MAKES 20 COOKIES

1 (7-ounce) tube almond paste (about ¾ cup)

5 large egg whites, divided

½ teaspoon baker's ammonia (*see page 163*) dissolved in 1 teaspoon water, or 1 teaspoon baking powder

Zest of 1 large lemon

⅓ cup finely chopped candied lemon peel

⅓ cup finely chopped candied orange peel

1 cup flour

1 cup finely ground hazelnuts, also known as hazelnut flour

1 cup finely ground almonds, also known as almond flour

1 tablespoon cinnamon

¾ teaspoon ground cloves

½ teaspoon ground anise seed, or ¼ teaspoon ground star anise

½ teaspoon ground coriander

3 tablespoons blanched, roughly chopped almonds

1⅓ cups plus 1 tablespoon sugar

Generous pinch kosher salt

20 round oblaten wafers, about 2½ inches in diameter

60 whole blanched almonds

Glaze

1¼ cups confectioner's sugar

1. To make the cookies, crumble almond paste into a stand mixer fitted with the paddle attachment. Add 1 egg white and mix on medium speed until very smooth and no lumps remain, 1 to 2 minutes. Add baker's ammonia or baking powder and mix on medium-low until well incorporated, about 15 seconds. Add lemon zest and candied lemon and orange peels and mix again just to combine. Transfer to a medium bowl and clean stand mixer bowl well (reserve paddle; do not clean).

2. In a medium bowl, whisk together flour, ground hazelnuts and almonds, cinnamon, cloves, anise, coriander, and chopped almonds.

3. In clean stand mixer bowl fitted with the whisk attachment, combine remaining 4 egg whites, sugar, and salt. Whip on medium-high speed until glossy and peaks form, about 3 to 4 minutes.

4. With reserved paddle, hand mash about ½ cup egg white mixture into almond paste mixture. It will be very stiff. Add another ½ cup egg whites and incorporate again. Transfer almond paste mixture to egg whites in stand mixer. Add flour-nut mixture and mix on medium speed until just combined, about 30 seconds, scraping down bowl and paddle if needed. Allow dough to rest, uncovered, for 30 minutes.

5. Line two baking sheets with parchment paper or Silpat mats and place 10 oblaten wafers on each. Place about 3 tablespoons dough on each wafer. With an offset spatula or blunt knife, spread dough to edges of wafer. It should be slightly mounded in center. Press 3 whole almonds in center of each, pointed ends facing outward like flower petals. Allow cookies to rest, uncovered, for 12 hours or overnight.

6. Preheat oven to 350° and place racks in top and bottom third of oven.

7. Bake cookies until speckled light brown in spots, about 18 to 20 minutes, rotating pans top to bottom and front to back halfway through. Remove from oven and glaze while still warm.

8. To make glaze, whisk together confectioner's sugar and 2 tablespoons of water in a small bowl. Use a pastry brush or your finger to spread glaze evenly on cookies to edges (cookies are sturdy enough to lift). Cool completely and wrap in plastic or store in food storage containers for up to 6 weeks.

VARIATIONS:

CHOCOLATE GLAZE: Combine 1 ounce unsweetened chocolate and 3 tablespoons water in a medium saucepan. Warm on medium heat until chocolate is melted, stirring regularly. Remove from heat and whisk in the confectioner's sugar. Add an additional 1 to 2 teaspoons of water if needed to create a smooth glaze.

UNGLAZED: Purists can leave out the blanched almonds and the glaze for a simple but very satisfying cookie.

CITRUS-DATE STOLLEN

In Dresden, the tradition of baking stollen, a bread-like fruitcake, for Christmas goes back more than five hundred years. Originally an oat cake, today's stollen is made with a combination of candied dried citrus, rum-soaked raisins, almonds, and often almond paste. If you can't find candied lemon peel (check with your local nut vendor or specialty baking shop during the holidays; it's also available online), substitute the same amount of mixed candied citrus or additional orange peel.

In this version, California dates give buttery stollen an almost caramel finish. Making two loaves at a time ensures you'll have enough to nibble in small slivers with espresso throughout the holiday season.

Note that soaking nuts like almonds overnight keeps them from wicking moisture away from the stollen. And baking on two stacked baking sheets (or an insulated baking sheet) keeps the bottom of the loaves from browning too quickly.

MAKES 2 LARGE LOAVES

⅔ cup black raisins

⅔ cup golden raisins

⅓ cup dark rum

1 cup slivered or roughly chopped almonds, lightly toasted (*see page 193*)

1 package (2¼ teaspoons) active dry yeast

½ cup whole milk, at room temperature

4 cups flour, divided

3 tablespoons sugar

½ teaspoon ginger

1 teaspoon ground cinnamon

1 teaspoon ground cardamom

1 teaspoon nutmeg

1 teaspoon kosher salt

1 teaspoon lemon zest

2 teaspoons vanilla bean paste or vanilla extract

1 cup (8 ounces) unsalted butter, melted

1 large egg yolk

1 cup chopped dates

½ cup finely chopped candied lemon peel

½ cup finely chopped candied orange peel

1. Mix together both raisins and rum in small, shallow bowl or food container. In another bowl, combine almonds and ¼ cup water. Cover and set aside at room temperature at least 3 hours or overnight.

2. In the bowl of a stand mixer fitted with the paddle attachment, combine yeast, milk, and 1 cup flour. Mix on low speed until a soft, sticky dough forms, about 2 minutes. Transfer starter to a lightly greased bowl, cover loosely, and set aside in a warm spot for 1 to 1½ hours. It should bubble on the surface. If not, discard and begin again with new yeast.

3. Clean the stand mixer bowl and add remaining 3 cups of flour, sugar, ginger, cinnamon, cardamom, nutmeg, and salt. Mix on low speed until just combined. Add lemon zest and vanilla bean paste or extract, return to low speed, and slowly pour in melted butter followed by egg yolk. Continue to mix for 30 seconds and add the yeast starter, ⅓ at a time, continuing to mix and scrape down paddle as needed. Increase speed to medium and mix until starter is fully incorporated and dough begins to look glossy, 4 to 5 minutes.

4. Add chopped dates, lemon and orange peels, and soaked almonds and raisins (if any water or rum remains, discard) to the dough. Mix on low speed until well combined, 2 to 3 minutes, and turn out onto a lightly floured work surface. Knead with your hands until dough begins to look slightly glossy and dried fruit is well incorporated, about 4 to 5 minutes. Transfer dough to a

medium bowl, cover with plastic, and set aside to rest in a warm spot for 1 hour. Reach into bowl, fold dough on itself 4 or 5 times like wrapping a package, cover, and set aside to rest for 1 more hour.

5. Stack 2 rimmed baking sheets on top of each other and line with parchment (or use an insulated baking sheet). Divide dough in half and shape each half into an oval about 8 inches long. Transfer to stacked baking sheets and set aside to rest, uncovered, in a warm spot for 1 to 1¼ hours. Dough will rise slightly but will not double.

6. Preheat oven to 350° and place rack in middle of oven. Bake loaves until tops are golden brown throughout and bottom is very dark golden brown, about 1 hour. If using a thermometer, internal temperature of loaves should read about 190°.

7. To glaze stollen, brush with 1 cup melted butter while the loaves are still warm. Do not move loaves; they fall apart easily when warm. After 30 minutes (when still warm), generously sprinkle loaves all over with the granulated sugar; use your hands to coat sugar onto the sides. Cover each loaf in plastic wrap and let rest overnight. The next day, sift confectioner's sugar over loaves, using your hands to press sugar onto the sides until the loaves have a ¼-inch thick crust of powdered sugar. Wrap each loaf in plastic wrap and allow to age at room temperature for 48 hours before serving. Store stollen at room temperature for one month or longer.

Glaze

1 cup (8 ounces) unsalted butter, melted

1 cup granulated sugar

1½ cups confectioners' sugar, more as needed

DAS DESSERT

THE CRAFTSMANSHIP OF DESSERT

I've always had a sweet tooth. Although I was classically trained as a chef and completed a rigorous apprenticeship in a Michelin-starred restaurant in the Black Forest, the part of the curriculum I was most fond of was dessert making.

It was during that time, when I was training to make desserts, that I began to appreciate the importance of balancing flavors and textures. As you will see in most of the recipes in this section, none are overly sweet. Instead, they have a subtle sweetness and are complemented by the tanginess of fruit, the crunchiness of ground nuts, or the tartness of quark. To me, the best desserts are not in-your-face sugar bombs; each is a well-crafted, well-tempered creation whose whole is better than the sum of its parts.

I'm sure I have, over the years, modified some of my desserts to adapt to the sweeter American palate, but I've really tried to remain true to the traditions of the great German and Viennese *kaffeehauses*, which offer a dozen or so varieties of cakes—some made with seasonal fruits, some offered year-round—displayed in a case near the entrance alongside daily baked apple-raisin strudel and fresh *schlag* (whipped cream). Although their menus almost always list desserts, it is not uncommon for guests to accompany the waiter to the case to make their selection—sometimes even pointing out the exact slice they want.

I've always looked forward to *kaffee und kuchen* time—the moment in the late afternoon, between meals, when I can take a break from kitchen work to sit down and indulge in a perfectly made slice of cake, washed down by sips of strong, rich coffee. It seems a luxury, but if you're ever in Germany or Vienna, I guarantee you, there's no better way to spend an afternoon.

KAISERSCHMARRN

Kaiserschmarrn is a classic Austrian pancake-like dessert with fruit toppings that vary with the seasons. Every home cook in Germany has his or her own version, but my good friend and chef de cuisine, Wolfgang Gussmack, makes by far the best version I've ever had.

MAKES 5 TO 6 SERVINGS

1. Preheat oven to 350°.

2. In a small saucepan, bring rum to a low simmer, add raisins, and remove from heat. Set aside.

3. In a large bowl, whisk together ¼ cup sugar and egg yolks. Whisk in milk until well combined.

4. In a stand mixer fitted with the whisk attachment or with a hand mixer, beat egg whites on medium-high speed until soft peaks form, about 1½ minutes. Add 1 tablespoon sugar and beat until whites are glossy, about 30 seconds.

5. Whisk half of egg whites into milk mixture, then about half of flour. Repeat with remaining egg whites and flour, whisking until flour is just incorporated but no longer.

6. In a 12-inch nonstick ovenproof skillet, heat butter over medium-high heat. Sprinkle remaining 1 tablespoon sugar over bottom of pan and cook until butter just begins to brown, about 1½ minutes. Pour batter into pan and reduce heat to medium-low. Strain raisins and sprinkle evenly on top. Cook until pancake is lightly browned on the bottom and beginning to set around the edges (small bubbles will form on top), 5 to 6 minutes.

7. Transfer pan to the oven and bake until center of pancake is just set, 12 to 15 minutes. Remove from oven and run a rubber spatula along the edges. To flip the pancake, lightly butter a large heatproof plate or unrimmed baking sheet and carefully place it on top of the skillet. Use oven mitts to flip the skillet so pancake is now on the plate, then slide the pancake back into pan (the bottom side will now be facing up). If the pancake breaks, just pile the pieces back into the pan. Return to oven and bake until it is set in the center but still moist, about 5 minutes.

8. Slice kaiserschmarrn into bite-size pieces and sprinkle with powdered sugar. Serve immediately with a fruit compote, if desired.

¼ cup rum

⅓ cup raisins

¼ cup plus 2 tablespoons sugar, divided

4 large eggs, separated

3 cups whole milk

2¼ cups flour, sifted

3 tablespoons (1½ ounces) unsalted butter, more for flipping pancake

¼ cup powdered sugar, sifted, for serving

Apple-Cinnamon or Pear–Star Anise Compote (*recipe page 187*), for serving (optional)

LINZERTORTE BARS

Patti always gets a kick out of telling the story about how stingy I used to be when it came to shar-ing my favorite pastries. For years each winter, my mom would carefully select the best-looking linzertorte she could find, slice it in half, pack one half atop the other, and send it on the 6,000-mile journey from Germany to California. As I unpacked the cake, I'd nibble every stray crumb, and then safely stash it on the highest shelf in the kitchen, just out of reach of Patti and the kids. Over the next month, I'd ration off slivers for all of us to enjoy.

Now that I make my own linzertortes at the bakery, I bake them in a square pan so they are easy to cut into (very portable) bars. And now I share more freely.

MAKES ABOUT 16 TO 20 BARS

2 cups finely ground hazelnuts, also known as hazelnut flour

1½ cups flour

2 tablespoons cocoa powder

1 teaspoon baking powder

¼ teaspoon kosher salt

1 cup (8 ounces) unsalted butter, room temperature, more for the pan

1¼ cups sugar

½ teaspoon lemon zest, packed

2 large eggs, divided

¾ cup good-quality raspberry jam

1 tablespoon Port, if needed

1. Preheat oven to 350°. Place rack in middle of oven. Butter a 9" x 9" baking pan, line the bottom with parchment paper, and lightly butter the top of the parchment.

2. In a large bowl, whisk together ground hazelnuts, flour, cocoa, baking powder, and salt.

3. In a stand mixer fitted with the paddle attachment, cream together butter, sugar, and lemon zest on medium speed until light and creamy, about 2 minutes. Add eggs, one at a time, mixing well between each addition. Scrape down sides of the bowl, add half of hazelnut-flour mixture, and mix on low speed until batter just comes together. Add remaining dry ingredients and mix well.

4. Place 1 rounded cup of batter in a medium, sealable food stor-age bag. Press out the air and seal the bag.

5. Spread remaining batter into prepared baking pan and roughly smooth the top with your fingers. Freeze for 15 minutes. If jam is very thick, place it in a small bowl and whisk in the Port. Spread jam on top of the chilled batter.

6. Snip about ½ inch off one bottom corner of the food storage bag to create an opening about ¾-inch wide (don't worry about exact measurements). Starting at one corner, gently squeeze the bag to pipe a diagonal line of batter down the center of the torte to the opposite corner. Pipe another diagonal line on each side of the center line so you have three evenly spaced, parallel lines. The crosshatch windows should be much wider than an

American-style pie; the batter is so thick, it spreads while baking (that's also why piping fewer lines on the bottom helps). To make a crosshatch pattern, pipe a diagonal line of batter down the center of the torte again, this time connecting the opposite two corners. Pipe two diagonal lines on each side of the center line. Use any remaining batter to connect any broken sections.

7. Place pan in oven and bake until edges are light golden brown and crosshatches in the center feel lightly springy to the touch, 34 to 38 minutes. The torte should be very moist; it will continue to set up as it cools.

8. Place the torte on a rack to cool for 15 minutes and run a knife around the edges of the pan to loosen the torte. Allow to cool completely and cut into 16 to 20 bars or squares.

ZWETSCHGENDATSCHI
(Prune Plum Tart)

There's nothing quite like the distinctly tart prune plums, which are at their best when cooked. There was a time when lucking into prune plums in California meant you knew someone with a tree in their backyard. Nowadays, you can often round up a case at farmers' markets and even some grocery stores; I've even seen them at Costco. The late summer harvest is short, so I buy huge quantities—a good 1,600 pounds or more—and halve, pit, and freeze them for year-round jam-making and for this fantastic streusel-cream tart. If you find them at your market, buy lots and freeze them, too. The tart really needs to feature prune plums, so I don't recommend substituting other kinds.

If using frozen plum halves, don't thaw them before baking (they will lose their shape and be more difficult to arrange in the pan). Give them a quick rinse under warm water to remove any ice, and lay them out on paper towels to dry for a few minutes before baking.

MAKES 12 SERVINGS

Dough

½ cup (4 ounces) unsalted butter, room temperature

¾ cup powdered sugar

¼ teaspoon baking powder

Pinch kosher salt

1 large egg white

¼ cup whole milk

1 teaspoon lemon zest, packed

2¼ cups flour, divided

Streusel

⅓ cup sugar

1⅓ cups flour

Pinch of kosher salt

¼ cup plus 2 tablespoons (3 ounces) unsalted butter, melted

Tart

1 to 2 tablespoons unsalted butter, for the tart pan

1 cup heavy cream

½ cup plain Greek-style yogurt or homemade quark (*recipe page 37*)

3 large eggs

½ teaspoon vanilla bean paste or vanilla extract

½ cup sugar

1. To make the tart dough, combine butter, powdered sugar, baking powder, salt, egg white, milk, and lemon zest in a stand mixer fitted with the paddle attachment. Mix on low speed until sugar is incorporated, about 30 seconds. Add about half the flour and mix again to combine. Add remaining flour and mix until dough comes together around the paddle, about 1 minute. Remove dough from stand mixer, shape into an approximately 5-inch disc, and wrap in plastic wrap. Refrigerate for 1 to 2 hours.

2. To make the streusel, whisk together sugar, flour, and salt in a medium bowl. Add melted butter and crumble the mixture together with your fingers.

3. Preheat the oven to 350°. Generously butter the bottom and sides of a 10-inch springform pan.

4. To assemble the tart, whisk together cream, yogurt or quark, eggs, vanilla bean paste or extract, sugar, and salt in a large bowl. Whisk in flour until no lumps remain.

5. Lightly dust a work surface with flour. Roll the dough into roughly a 14-inch circle, lightly flouring top of the dough as needed. Gently fold the dough in half and transfer it to the pan, pressing dough lightly around the sides and corners. Trim away pieces of dough that hang over the top of the pan and use the trimmings to patch up any holes. No need to crimp or finish the edges—this tart has a rustic look.

6. Starting at the edge of the pan, arrange the oval plum halves in concentric rows so they stand up "at attention" like little soldiers. Try to use the largest plum halves on the outermost row and the smaller ones on the second row. Arrange 3 or 4 plum halves decoratively in the middle and pour cream mixture evenly over plums. Sprinkle the tart with the sugar-flour streusel mixture. Press down lightly to adhere the topping.

7. Bake the tart until the edges of the crust are golden brown and the cream filling barely jiggles when pan is gently shaken, 1 hour and 30 minutes (check after 1 hour and 15 minutes). Transfer tart to a wire rack to cool for 10 minutes. Warm the jam for about 15 seconds in the microwave or on the stovetop to slightly soften it. Use a pastry brush to brush jam over the outermost 3 inches of the tart so you have a wide, circular ring of glaze (some of the streusel will not stay in place; that's fine). Sprinkle toasted almonds on top of the jam and allow the tart to cool completely.

8. Just before serving, sift powdered sugar lightly over the almonds. Slice the tart into 12 pieces (wipe off the blade between slices with a paper towel if the cream filling sticks to the knife). Cover in plastic wrap and store at room temperature up to 3 days.

Pinch kosher salt

½ cup flour, more for rolling out dough

About 28 to 30 medium, pitted prune plums, sliced in half lengthwise

½ cup good-quality apricot jam

½ cup sliced almonds, toasted (*see page 193*)

1 to 2 tablespoons powdered sugar

How to Freeze Prune Plums

Line several baking sheets with plastic wrap. Slice plums in half lengthwise and remove the pits. Place plums in a single layer on baking sheets and freeze until they harden. Transfer to food storage bags and freeze for up to 6 months.

Dark Chocolate Hazelnut Cake

MOHR IM HEMD
(Dark Chocolate Hazelnut Cake)

Most Americans think of German chocolate cake as a milk chocolate layer cake with a coconut–pecan icing. Other than the name, there's nothing German about it. In the 1950s, a home baker in Texas invented the cake using a brand of chocolate called German's Sweet Chocolate.

Mohr im Hemd, which has Austrian roots, is a cross between flourless dark chocolate cake and hazelnut sponge cake that is baked in a water bath like a crème brûlée. The result is a very moist, almost creamy dark chocolate cake. If you have classic mini bundt cake molds, this is the time to pull them out (you can also bake the cakes in ramekins). The hole in the middle serves as a handy pocket to pile on the ice cream or whipped cream.

MAKES 6 INDIVIDUAL CAKES

½ cup (4 ounces) unsalted butter, room temperature, additional for coating molds

⅔ cup sugar, divided

6 large eggs, yolks and whites separated, room temperature

4 ounces unsweetened chocolate, melted and slightly cooled

1¼ cups hazelnut flour

⅓ cup toasted, unseasoned bread-crumbs (*recipe page 21*)

Generous pinch kosher salt

To serve

Vanilla ice cream or lightly sweet-ened whipped cream

Chocolate Sauce (*recipe page 183*)

Chopped, toasted hazelnuts (*see page 193*), for garnish

1. Preheat oven to 350° and place rack in middle of oven. Lightly butter a baking sheet.

2. Generously grease a 6-mold mini bundt (8 ounces each) sheet pan with butter, working butter into every nook, and set aside. Place a 9" x 13" baking dish in oven and fill with about 1½ inches water. Alternatively, butter 6 large (8-ounce) ramekins and set aside, then place a large roasting pan (or 2 smaller pans; ramekins won't fit in a 9" x 13" pan) in oven and fill with about 1 inch water.

3. In a stand mixer fitted with the paddle attachment, cream butter and ⅓ cup sugar on medium speed until well combined, about 1 minute. With mixer running, add 3 egg yolks, mix until well incorporated, and scrape down sides of bowl. Repeat with remaining 3 yolks. Add melted chocolate (it should not be hot), and mix until smooth. Add hazelnut flour, breadcrumbs, and salt and mix again until well incorporated, scraping down sides of bowl as needed. Set aside.

4. Replace paddle with whisk attachment and switch to a clean mixer bowl (or transfer chocolate to a medium bowl, and wash and dry mixer bowl well). Add all 6 egg whites and remaining ⅓ cup sugar and beat on high until stiff and glossy but not dry, about 1½ minutes.

5. Fold ⅓ of egg whites into chocolate mixture and mix well with a rubber spatula. Add another ⅓ of egg whites, this time gently folding in a circular motion from bottom of bowl to the top to

avoid deflating whites. Add final ⅓ of egg whites and continue to gently mix until just combined. Flecks of egg white should be visible. Immediately divide mixture evenly among mini bundt molds or ramekins. Carefully place bundt mold pan or ramekins in hot water–filled baking pan in oven. Bake until tops are lightly springy to the touch and a cake tester comes out clean, about 18 to 20 minutes. If baking in ceramic ramekins, allow 2 to 3 minutes longer. Carefully remove bundt pan or ramekins from water bath and cool for 2 to 3 minutes.

6. Place buttered baking sheet on top of bundt pan and flip upside down to remove cakes. For ramekins, place a small plate on top of each, flip each over, and place cakes right side up on buttered sheet pan. Allow cakes to cool for 2 to 3 minutes. Top with ice cream or whipped cream, chocolate sauce, and chopped hazelnuts, and serve immediately.

7. If making ahead, when completely cool, cover cakes with plastic wrap and refrigerate for up to 3 days. Before serving, bring to room temperature and re-warm in a 300° oven for 4 to 5 minutes.

CHOCOLATE SAUCE

I use this sauce in the Mohr im Hemd above, but don't limit yourself to just that. It's a versatile go-to chocolate sauce that can be made in advance and enjoyed with a great number of desserts.

MAKES 2 CUPS

1 cup heavy cream

8 ounces semi-sweet chocolate, roughly chopped, or chocolate chips

Pinch cinnamon

1. Warm cream in a medium saucepan over medium-low heat until warm to the touch. Add chocolate and cinnamon and whisk constantly until chocolate is melted, 3 to 4 minutes. Immediately remove sauce from the heat. Serve immediately, or allow sauce to cool completely, refrigerate for up to 5 days, and gently re-warm before serving.

KÄSEKUCHEN *(Cheesecake)*

I've been making this cheesecake—more of an elegant tart, really—for years. I wanted to merge the best qualities of German and American cheesecakes (no small task, as both sides of the cheesecake world tend to be very opinionated). In the German style, this one is not too sweet, and the filling has the silkier texture of an American-style cheesecake. But it's the tangy crème fraîche topping that really pulls everything—and everyone, I hope—together. If you don't have fresh berries for the topping, any chunky fruit sauce or compote (a cranberry sauce during the holidays would be lovely) will work fine.

Graham crackers are easy to grind in a food processor—just pick out any big pieces that remain and smash them by hand.

MAKES 10 TO 12 SERVINGS

Crust

6 ounces graham crackers, finely ground (about 1½ cups)

3 tablespoons sugar

½ teaspoon cinnamon

Pinch ground cloves

½ cup (4 ounces) unsalted butter, melted, more for buttering pan

Filling

1 pound cream cheese, room temperature

8 ounces mascarpone cheese, room temperature

⅓ cup sugar

2 teaspoons vanilla extract

3 large eggs, lightly beaten

Topping

8 ounces (about 1 cup) crème fraîche or sour cream

1½ tablespoons sugar

½ teaspoon vanilla extract

To serve

Fresh blackberries, raspberries, or prepared or homemade fruit sauce or compote (optional)

1. Preheat oven to 300°. Grease bottom and sides of a 10-inch springform pan generously with butter.

2. To make the crust, mix together graham cracker crumbs, sugar, cinnamon, cloves, and melted butter in a small bowl. Press about ¼ to ⅓ of crumbs around sides of pan about 1 inch high. Firmly press remaining crumbs in the bottom of the pan.

3. To make the filling, in the bowl of a stand mixer fitted with the paddle attachment, combine cream cheese, mascarpone, sugar, and vanilla. Beat on medium speed until fluffy, about 3 to 4 minutes. Add eggs and beat until smooth, about 1 minute, scraping down sides of bowl halfway through. Scrape filling into prepared crust and use a rubber spatula to roughly smooth the top.

4. Bake cheesecake until center is just set but jiggles slightly when pan is shaken, 32 to 36 minutes. To test, butter one finger and gently touch center of cake; it should be set but give slightly. Place cheesecake on a rack to cool for 30 minutes (leave the oven on).

5. Meanwhile, make the topping. In a small bowl, whisk together crème fraîche or sour cream, sugar, and vanilla. After cake has cooled for 30 minutes, pour topping over cheesecake and spread evenly over the top with an offset spatula. Return cake to oven and bake for 10 minutes. The topping will look a little glossy but will not significantly change in texture. Cool cheesecake completely on a wire rack (at least 2 hours). Cover cake with plastic wrap and refrigerate overnight.

6. To serve, remove sides from the springform pan. Cut cheese-cake into 10 to 12 slices with a sharp knife, dipping the knife blade in warm water between slices and wiping off any cream cheese with a paper towel. Serve cheesecake on its own or with fresh berries or sauce. Refrigerate for up to 4 days.

MARINATED CHERRIES WITH ELDERFLOWER SABAYON

The local sour cherry cakes, pies, and liqueur in the Black Forest region where I grew up are deserving of their fame. The sweet cherries you find at the height of summer in California are also delicious, especially if you eat them when really fresh. Dressed up with a little kirsch and elderflower-scented sabayon, these cherries make me feel like I'm sitting at an outdoor café in Berlin in the summertime.

For the sabayon, you can find elderflower syrup at German and many other specialty European markets, or substitute the hazelnut- or almond-flavored syrups you see in the coffee aisle at well-stocked grocery stores. The only trick is to whisk the sabayon constantly and vigorously to get a silky texture. It's fantastic on any stone fruit or berries.

===== MAKES 4 SERVINGS =====

1 pound fresh cherries, pitted

2 tablespoons kirsch

¼ teaspoon cinnamon

4 large egg yolks

⅓ cup elderflower syrup (or hazelnut or almond syrup)

½ cup dry white wine, such as sauvignon blanc

2 to 3 fresh mint leaves, torn into small pieces, or ¼ cup finely chopped, toasted almonds (*see page 195*)

1. In a medium bowl, toss together cherries, kirsch, and cinnamon. Set aside.

2. Fill a medium saucepan about ⅓ full of water and choose a medium metal bowl that fits snugly on top but does not touch the water. Remove bowl and bring the water to a simmer.

3. Whisk together eggs, elderflower syrup, and wine. When water simmers, place bowl on top of the saucepan and whisk vigorously and constantly in a circular motion, scraping the bottom of the pan so the eggs do not curdle. Within 3 to 4 minutes, the egg mixture should become very frothy and rise noticeably in the bowl, then recede and thicken to the consistency of a light cream sauce (it should still have little air bubbles). Carefully remove the bowl from the heat with a kitchen towel.

4. If not serving immediately, transfer sabayon to a clean bowl and place a piece of plastic wrap directly on top of the sauce, so it doesn't create a film as it cools. Set aside at room temperature for up to 2 hours. Whisk again just before serving.

5. To serve, pile cherries into 4 or 5 serving bowls and spoon the sabayon on top. Sprinkle with mint or almonds.

APPLE-CINNAMON OR PEAR–STAR ANISE COMPOTE

Spoon either compote, really more similar to poached fruit, on desserts or on top of yogurt or ice cream. Save any leftover braising liquid to add to soda water or cocktails.

YIELD 3½ TO 4 CUPS

1. Use a vegetable peeler to peel 3 sections of peel (avoid pith), about 4 to 5 inches long each, from lemons. Slice lemons in half and squeeze juice through a strainer into a medium bowl. Add sliced apples or pears to bowl and toss to combine.

2. To make the apple-cinnamon compote, combine 1½ cups water, lemon peels, apple juice, sugar, and cinnamon stick in a medium saucepan with tall sides and a lid. To make the pear–star anise compote, substitute star anise for the cinnamon and pears for the apples and do the same thing.

3. Bring mixture to a low boil, stir once to make sure sugar is dissolved, and add apples and lemon juice or pears and lemon juice. Return mixture to a simmer, immediately turn off heat, and allow compote to cool completely in the pan. Transfer to a bowl or storage container and top apples or pears with enough braising liquid to cover (save any remaining liquid for drinks). Refrigerate overnight to allow flavors to develop. Remove lemon peels and spices, and serve the sliced fruit chilled and topped with a small amount of braising liquid. Refrigerate for up to 1 week.

2 medium lemons

4 large, tangy apples, such as Granny Smith or Gravenstein, sliced, or

4 large, firm pears (such as Anjou), peeled, cored, and sliced (about 1⅓ pounds)

1 cup good-quality apple juice

¼ cup sugar

1 cinnamon stick (for apples) or 2 star anise (for pears)

ACHT

PANTRY

COMMON INGREDIENTS

PRODUCE

Celery Root (Celeriac)

Celery root, also known as celeriac, has a long history in Northern European cooking. The knobby root end of this celery variety has a delicate flavor, almost a subtle cross between parsley and celery. The texture is similar to its cousin, the turnip, but celeriac manages to achieve so much more when puréed or simmered in soups and stews. Look for firm bulbs with bright green stems and no soft spots on the skin. Discard the stems; though they look like celery, they typically have a very bitter flavor.

HOW TO PEEL CELERIAC: Use a sharp paring knife to slice off both ends, and then trim off the thick, knobby skin to reveal the firm, white flesh. Like artichokes, the vegetable will begin to turn brown almost immediately. To preserve the color, place peeled celeriac immediately in a medium bowl of water with the juice of half a lemon.

Parsnips

I love parsnips for their understated elegance and sweet, nutty flavor. They can be bitter when raw but are excellent simmered in soups, quickly stir-fried, or grated into a savory pancake batter. Like carrots (the two are related), parsnips should be firm to the touch. Most parsnips available at grocery stores are very large and need to be peeled and cored. If you find small, tender baby parsnips at the farmers' market, you don't need to peel or core them. Just scrub them well and trim off the stems.

HOW TO PEEL AND CORE LARGE PARSNIPS: After peeling with a vegetable peeler, slice off both ends of the parsnips. Use a small paring knife to slice away the flesh of the parsnip from

the firm, white core in the center (like coring a pineapple). If a little core remains, that's fine.

Potatoes

Potatoes are available in so many different varieties today, from tiny fingerlings to the more common large russets. Use starchier potatoes like russets for mashing and waxier varieties like new potatoes for roasting.

TO PREPARE POTATOES: Always scrub potatoes well before cooking to remove any dirt. When I'm making dishes like classic German potato salad *(recipe page 80)*, I like to boil small potatoes whole with the skin on (to retain the most flavor and nutrients), until tender but still firm. After straining the potatoes, peel them while they are still warm.

Radishes

Radishes, a common ingredient in German cooking, come in a wide range of shapes, sizes, and flavors, from small, round butter radishes to large, white Japanese radishes that resemble daikon. One of my favorite preparations is the simplest: Thinly slice the best market radishes and arrange them atop a thick slice of country

bread with plenty of good butter and a sprinkle of sea salt.

TO PREPARE RADISHES: Thoroughly wash away any dirt and serve radishes whole, sliced, or chopped.

Rhubarb

Rhubarb is revered in Europe, where it is canned and preserved or used in pies and tarts. When I first moved here, I couldn't find it much, but that has really changed in the last few years. When cooked with a little sugar, the vegetable takes on a fantastically sweet, tart, almost berry-like flavor. The rhubarb available at supermarkets tends to be large, thick stalks that resemble pink celery stalks. At farmers' markets, you may find some of the tender, baby stalks in springtime. Both work well.

TO PREPARE RHUBARB: Trim both ends and roughly chop the rhubarb before simmering or baking in some sort of liquid (to keep it moist).

SPICES

Look for good-quality spices at retail stores or such online spice vendors as Penzeys and Pendery's.

Anise Seed

Anise seed is not the same as star anise, which has a stronger licorice flavor. If you have only star anise, use half the amount.

Bay Leaves

Fresh bay leaves have a more restrained flavor than dried. You can find them at some farmers' markets, or substitute half the quantity of dried leaves.

Caraway

Traditionally used in rye breads, sauerkraut, and other fermented dishes, caraway seeds add a distinct slightly sweet and peppery flavor. I often add them to the boiling water when making potato salads, or sprinkle them on baked potatoes with homemade quark.

Coriander

The seeds of the cilantro plant have an almost citrusy flavor that's quite different from the fresh leaves. In Germany, they are often used in ground form in traditional holiday spice mixes, along with such spices as cinnamon, cloves, anise, and ginger.

Juniper Berries

The dried berries of the juniper tree have a subtle pine flavor. In Germany, they're used to flavor stews and game meats like goose. I like to add them to sauerkraut and Citrus-Spiced Red Cabbage *(see recipe page 78)*. They also add a distinct flavor to Black Forest ham. To release their flavor, lightly crush the berries with a mortar and pestle or place them on a work surface and lightly smash the berries with a heavy-bottomed skillet.

Tarragon

With its anise-like flavor, tarragon works well in vinegars and marinades. A little goes a long way. The leaves lose much of their flavor when dried, so substitute fresh marjoram if you can't find fresh tarragon.

FLOURS

BREAD FLOUR

Bread flour has a higher amount of protein than all-purpose flour, and that protein helps rustic breads like sourdough develop a good gluten structure and their signature slightly chewy texture. You can find it at most well-stocked grocery stores.

RYE FLOUR

In Germany, *roggenmehl* (rye flour) is available in a wide variety of grain types and textures, from very light, finely ground rye flours to dark, coarsely ground grains. Here, look for rye flours labeled "medium" or "dark" to use in the bread recipes.

NUT FLOURS

German bakers often use finely ground nut flours to add flavor and moisture to baked goods. You can find finely ground hazelnuts and almonds, also called hazelnut or almond "flour," at most well-stocked grocery stores and specialty markets.

BASIC COOKING TECHNIQUES

TO ROAST BELL PEPPERS

Preheat oven to 450°. Rub 2 bell peppers generously with olive oil and place on a baking sheet. Roast the peppers until very soft and skin is blistered and charred in spots, 35 to 40 minutes, flipping peppers once or twice. Place peppers in a small bowl, cover tightly with plastic wrap, and set aside to cool for 15 minutes. Peel peppers and discard the skin, seeds, and stems.

TO POACH EGGS

Crack 4 eggs into each of 4 small ramekins. Fill a medium saucepan with about 3 inches of water. Bring water to a gentle simmer and add 1 tablespoon distilled white vinegar or white wine vinegar. One at a time, place the edge of a ramekin near simmering water and carefully slide eggs into the water. Cook until egg whites are firm and yolk is set but still runny, 3 to 4 minutes. Remove eggs with a slotted spoon, gently blot dry with a paper towel, and serve immediately.

TO GRATE AN APPLE

Grate a washed, unpeeled apple on the largest holes of a box grater, starting on one side and grating down toward the core. Discard any large pieces of skin that come off as you work. Move to the next side of the apple and repeat until all 4 sides have been grated and you are left with the core.

TO TOAST NUTS

Preheat oven to 350°. Spread out whole or roughly chopped nuts in a single layer on a rimmed baking sheet and bake until lightly toasted, about 7 to 10 minutes, stirring 2 or 3 times to evenly brown. Watch closely the last few minutes to avoid burning. Immediately transfer to a bowl or plate to cool.

TO TOAST SMALL SEEDS (LIKE SESAME SEEDS) OR SPICES

Heat a heavy-bottomed skillet over medium-high heat. Add spices in a single layer and toast, stirring regularly, until fragrant and just beginning to color, 2 to 3 minutes. Immediately transfer to a bowl or plate to cool.

STOCKS

HAM STOCK

This old-school stock is the ham equivalent of making stock from your leftover Thanksgiving turkey. Save the bones and meaty remnants from a whole ham, or use store-bought ham hocks.

MAKES ABOUT 3 QUARTS

1½ pounds meaty ham bones, meat, and rind from a whole ham, or store-bought ham hocks

1 medium onion, peeled and sliced in half

1 large carrot, peeled and roughly chopped

½ medium celery root, peeled and roughly chopped, or 2 medium stalks celery

1 dried bay leaf

8 peppercorns

1 tablespoon kosher salt, more to taste

1. In a large stockpot, combine 4 quarts water, ham leftovers or hocks, onion, carrot, celery root or celery, bay leaf, peppercorns, and salt. Bring to a boil, reduce heat, and simmer, uncovered, until stock takes on the light-yellow color of chicken stock, about 1 hour.

2. Cool stock completely and strain into a large bowl, pressing down on ham and vegetables to release the juices. Discard the solids. Season stock with additional salt to taste and allow to cool. Refrigerate stock until fat slightly congeals, about 2 hours. Skim off fat with a slotted spoon and discard. Refrigerate for up to 5 days or freeze in small batches.

BROWN VEAL STOCK

A dark, slow-roasted veal stock takes some time to make, yes, but it adds such a rich, distinct flavor to so many dishes and works well as a lazy-weekend time commitment. Start by slow-roasting the bones one morning, and finish up the stock later that day or the next morning. I usually order cracked veal bones from my butcher and make a big batch to freeze in small quantities. If you don't have an 8- to 10-quart stockpot, you'll need to cut the recipe in half or use a large, tall pasta pot. And don't be tempted to substitute beef bones for veal, as the stock will have a very different flavor. If you don't want to use veal, brown chicken stock works better as a substitute (recipe next page).

If you're using a portion of the stock to make glace de viande, a condensed veal syrup (recipe next page), omit the salt and season any remaining broth later or it will be too salty. Good-quality versions of glace de viande are available at specialty shops or online.

MAKES ABOUT 5 QUARTS STOCK

About 8 pounds cracked veal bones

2 large onions, peeled and roughly chopped into 1-inch pieces

2 medium carrots, peeled and sliced into 1-inch pieces

½ medium celery root, peeled and roughly chopped, or 2 medium stalks celery, sliced into 1-inch pieces

2 tablespoons tomato paste

2 cloves garlic, peeled

2 sprigs thyme

2 sprigs parsley

2 dried bay leaves

1 tablespoon whole black peppercorns

1 tablespoon kosher salt, or to taste (omit if making glace de viande)

1. Preheat oven to 400°. Place veal bones in a large roasting pan and roast until bones are well browned, about 1½ hours. Remove from oven, add onions, carrots, celery root or celery, and tomato paste. Use tongs to carefully spread vegetables around roasting pan (pan will be very hot) and loosen any bones that have caramelized and may be attached to bottom of pan. Return pan to oven and roast until vegetables are golden brown, about 1 more hour, stirring once or twice.

2. Place roasting pan on the stove and transfer bones to an 8- to 10-quart stockpot or tall pasta pot. Add ½ cup water to vegetables and pan juices in roasting pan to deglaze, scraping up any brown bits on the bottom with a spatula. Add pan juice to the stockpot along with garlic, thyme, parsley, bay leaves, peppercorns, and enough water to cover bones (about 6 to 7 quarts). Bring to a boil, reduce heat, and simmer, uncovered, for 2½ to 3 hours. Stock should be a rich golden brown color. If using only as stock, add salt to taste and allow to cool completely. If making glace de viande, omit salt.

3. Once stock has cooled completely, strain into a large bowl, pressing down on vegetables to release juices. Season with additional salt to taste and refrigerate stock until fat slightly congeals, 2 to 3 hours. Skim off fat with a slotted spoon and discard. Use stock within 3 to 4 days, or freeze in small batches in food storage bags.

BROWN CHICKEN STOCK

Follow the Brown Veal Stock recipe except as follows: Save raw bones, wings, and necks when cutting up whole chickens, or ask your butcher for bones. (Unlike veal bones, they will have some skin and cartilage attached.) Skip the first bone-only roasting step in the veal stock recipe and roast raw chicken bones with the vegetables for 1 hour. Then follow the rest of the instructions for making veal stock.

GLACE DE VIANDE

Place 4 cups unsalted veal or chicken stock in a medium saucepan, bring to a boil, and cook until stock is reduced to about ½ cup, about 1 hour or longer. Cool completely, and refrigerate for up to 1 week or freeze in very small batches (ice cube trays work well).

CONDIMENTS & SAUCES

HONEY MUSTARD

Make both a sweet and spicy mustard to serve with homemade pretzels (see recipe page 16) and everyone at your weekend tailgate—or in my case, tennis match—will be happy.

MAKES ABOUT ½ CUP

¼ cup whole-grain German mustard, such as Ingelhoffer

¼ cup Dijon mustard, such as Grey Poupon

2 tablespoons honey, warmed in the microwave for about 5 seconds or on the stovetop if stiff

1. Place both mustards and honey in a small bowl and mix well. Refrigerate for up to 1 week.

SPICY HORSERADISH MUSTARD

A good companion to the honey mustard.

MAKES ABOUT ½ CUP

⅓ cup Dijon mustard, such as Grey Poupon

2½ tablespoons American-style yellow mustard, such as French's

2 teaspoons horseradish, more to taste

1. Place both mustards and horseradish in a small bowl and mix well. Add additional horseradish to taste. Refrigerate for up to 1 week.

HERB MAYONNAISE

If you have any leftovers of this tangy herb mayonnaise, whisk in more lemon juice to make an instant salad dressing. You can swap in basil or other herbs for the tarragon.

MAKES ABOUT ¾ CUP

2 large egg yolks

1½ tablespoons freshly squeezed lemon juice

1 teaspoon Dijon mustard

¼ teaspoon kosher salt, more to taste

¾ cup vegetable oil, divided

1½ tablespoons finely chopped tarragon, marjoram, or basil leaves

Finely ground pepper (white or black), to taste

1. In a blender, combine egg yolks, lemon juice, mustard, and salt and blend until well combined. With blender running, very slowly drizzle ¼ cup vegetable oil into egg mixture, drop by drop. When

mixture begins to emulsify, slowly pour in remaining ½ cup oil until mixture thickens like a mayonnaise. Transfer to a food storage container and stir in whatever herb you're using. Season with additional salt and pepper to taste. Refrigerate for up to 3 days.

CHIPOTLE AIOLI

A quick, back-pocket aioli to spice up turkey sandwiches, burgers, or our Blackened Tomato Sandwich (see recipe page 61).

MAKES ABOUT 1 CUP

1 large egg yolk

½ teaspoon Dijon mustard

1 tablespoon freshly squeezed lemon juice

1 tablespoon freshly squeezed lime juice

1 tablespoon roughly chopped canned chipotles in adobo

½ teaspoon coarse sea or kosher salt, more to taste

¾ cup vegetable oil, divided

1. In a blender, combine egg yolk, mustard, lemon and lime juices, and chipotle and blend until well combined. With blender running, very slowly drizzle ¼ cup vegetable oil into egg mixture, drop by drop. When mixture begins to emulsify, slowly pour in remaining ½ cup oil until mixture thickens into a mayonnaise. Transfer to a food storage container and season with additional salt to taste. Refrigerate for up to 3 days.

JALAPEÑO RAISIN CHUTNEY

A spicy chutney for lamb burgers (see recipe page 118) *or just about any sandwich. Adjust the heat to your taste by using more or less jalapeño.*

MAKES ABOUT 1½ CUPS

1½ tablespoons vegetable oil

1 medium onion, finely chopped

1 jalapeño, stemmed, seeded, and finely chopped, or to taste

½ cup golden raisins

½ cup dark raisins

½ teaspoon crushed red pepper flakes, or to taste

1 tablespoon packed brown sugar

¼ teaspoon kosher salt, more to taste

Zest of 1 large lemon

3 tablespoons freshly squeezed lemon juice

½ cup good-quality apple cider or apple juice

1. In a large, heavy-bottomed saucepan, heat oil over medium heat. Add onion and sauté until translucent, 3 to 4 minutes. Add jalapeño and sauté 1 minute longer, stirring occasionally. Add both raisins, chile flakes, brown sugar, salt, lemon zest, and lemon juice and stir to combine. Pour cider or juice over mixture, bring to a simmer, and cook until liquid has mostly reduced but raisins are still plump and moist, about 15 minutes. Allow to cool completely and pulse mixture in a food processor about 4 or 5 times for a chunkier chutney, a few more times for a smoother chutney. Season with additional salt to taste. Refrigerate for up to 10 days.

SPICED TOMATO JAM

We slather this chunky tomato jam on our chicken club sandwich (recipe page 74), but it's also great on a burger or grilled cheese, or spread atop goat cheese as an appetizer.

Most supermarket tomatoes are too firm to work in this jam—not to mention not very flavorful—so ask for "seconds" (overripe and often bruised tomatoes) at your farmers' market. They're packed with flavor and soft enough to smash with your hands—and usually a bargain. You can omit the juniper berries, but if you have them, they add a nice woodsy flavor.

Note: This jam does not have enough acid to safely can and preserve, so use it within 10 days.

MAKES I TO 1¼ CUPS

2 pounds very ripe "seconds" heirloom tomatoes

½ cup red wine vinegar

½ cup brown sugar

¼ teaspoon crushed red pepper flakes, or
  ½ teaspoon for a spicier jam

½ teaspoon kosher salt

⅛ teaspoon ground cloves

2 juniper berries, lightly crushed (*see page 191*)

1 fresh bay leaf or about ½ dried bay leaf
  (do not crumble)

1. Working over a large bowl, remove stems and any blemishes and rough spots from tomatoes. Discard any skin that slips off while you work; any skin that remains is fine. Smash tomatoes with your fingers into 1-inch pieces. You should have about 3 cups of tomatoes and juice.

2. Transfer tomatoes and juice to a large, heavy-bottomed saucepan. Add vinegar, sugar, chile flakes, salt, cloves, juniper berries, and bay leaf and bring to a low boil over medium-high heat. Reduce to simmer and cook for 45 minutes to 1 hour (time will depend on the moisture content of tomatoes; most of juice should evaporate, though there should still be some in the bottom of the pan). Stir occasionally the first 30 minutes and then more frequently the final 15 to 30 minutes, scraping the bottom of the pan to avoid burning. Mixture should thicken but still look "juicy"; jam will thicken more as it cools. Remove bay leaf and set jam aside to cool completely. Refrigerate for up to 10 days.

FIRE-ROASTED SALSA

With plenty of olive oil, this salsa is almost like a sauce. It's great with Avocado Fries (see recipe page 95) or spooned over grilled or roasted fish. I like to use local lemons instead of limes, and be sure to use a firm tomato variety like romas. The liquid in juicy tomatoes will prevent the vegetables from caramelizing.

MAKES ABOUT 1¾ CUPS

2 large cloves garlic, roughly chopped

½ large onion, roughly chopped

1 large poblano chile, stemmed, seeded, and roughly chopped

1 medium jalapeño, stemmed, seeded, and roughly chopped, or to taste

4 large, firm roma tomatoes, sliced in half

4 tablespoons extra-virgin olive oil, divided

½ teaspoon kosher salt, divided, more to taste

½ large bunch cilantro, both tender top stems and leaves, roughly chopped (about 1 cup, packed)

1½ tablespoons freshly squeezed lemon juice, more to taste

1. Preheat oven to 400° and place rack in bottom third of oven.

2. Scatter garlic, onion, poblano, jalapeño, and tomatoes on a large, rimmed baking sheet. Toss them with 2 tablespoons olive oil and ¼ teaspoon salt and arrange tomatoes cut-side down on baking sheet. Roast until vegetables are lightly browned in places and tomatoes have begun to collapse, 30 to 35 minutes, stirring two or three times. Remove vegetables from oven and scrape any brown bits from bottom of pan with a spatula (stir them back into vegetables). Discard any tomato skins that fall off as you work. Allow to cool for 20 minutes.

3. Transfer roasted vegetables and any accumulated juices to a food processor. Add remaining ¼ teaspoon salt, cilantro, lemon juice, and remaining 2 tablespoons olive oil. For a chunkier salsa, pulse a few times and scrape down the sides of the bowl. For a smoother sauce, purée mixture until well combined. Season with additional salt and lemon juice to taste.

ROMESCO SAUCE

Traditional Spanish romesco sauces rely on a bread base. Here, along with the almonds, tomato paste adds body and flavor, and sherry vinegar and lemon juice give the sauce a tangy balance. Because I use romesco for so many things during the week, this recipe makes a generous amount. It's great as a sandwich spread, drizzled on top of white beans with a little olive oil, spooned on roasted chicken for a quick supper, and simply slathered on bread with a little cheese.

To freeze leftovers, spread the sauce flat in a food storage bag so you can easily break off little chunks as needed.

MAKES ABOUT 1¼ CUPS

¾ ounce dried ancho chiles (about 2 medium), stemmed, seeded, and torn into 2 or 3 pieces

¼ cup sherry vinegar

¼ cup extra-virgin olive oil

½ cup sliced almonds, lightly toasted (*see page 193*)

1 medium red bell pepper, roasted (*see page 193*), peeled, and torn into 2-inch pieces

2 medium cloves garlic, roughly chopped

1 tablespoon tomato paste

1 tablespoon paprika

⅛ teaspoon cayenne pepper

½ teaspoon kosher salt, more to taste

2 tablespoons freshly squeezed lemon juice, more to taste

1. Heat a medium, heavy-bottomed saucepan over medium-high heat. Add chiles to the pan a few pieces at a time and toast, flipping once, until chiles begin to deepen in color and smell toasty, 20 to 30 seconds per side (press down on them with tongs or a spatula slightly if needed). Transfer chiles to small bowl, fill with warm water, and set aside to soak for 10 minutes.

2. Drain chiles and add to blender with vinegar, olive oil, almonds, roasted pepper, garlic, tomato paste, paprika, cayenne, and salt. Purée until a thick paste forms, scraping sides of blender if necessary. Add lemon juice, mix to combine, and season with additional lemon juice and salt to taste. Refrigerate up to 1 week or freeze.

QUICK CARAMELIZED ONIONS

·

MAKES ABOUT 1 CUP

1 tablespoon unsalted butter

1 tablespoon extra-virgin olive oil

1 medium onion, thinly sliced

1 tablespoon sugar

3 to 4 tablespoons water, as needed

Kosher salt and freshly ground pepper, to taste

1. In a medium saucepan, heat butter and olive oil over medium-high heat. Add onions and sauté until just beginning to brown, 4 to 6 minutes. Add sugar and 2 tablespoons water and stir to combine. Continue to cook onions, stirring occasionally, until golden brown, 8 to 10 minutes. If onions appear dry, add 1 to 2 additional tablespoons of water, as needed, and scrape bottom of pan with a spatula to remove brown bits. Remove onions from heat and season with salt and pepper to taste.

GIARDINIERA

This spicy Italian condiment for salads and sandwiches is easy to make with grocery-store staples. Brining the vegetables in a salt cure tenderizes them just enough without taking away the crunch. I prefer to use rice vinegar, which is more subtly flavored than red or white wine vinegar. The giardiniera keeps well for several weeks (make sure the vegetables are completely submerged in the marinade), so I always make a picnic-friendly quantity. Brush the leftover marinade on grilled bread or fish—or use it for a second batch of giardiniera.

MAKES 12 TO 16 SERVINGS

Brined Vegetables

½ cup kosher salt

¼ cup unseasoned rice vinegar

1 medium cauliflower, broken into 1-inch florets (about 5 to 6 cups)

2 stalks celery, sliced into ¼-inch half moons

1 medium red bell pepper, thinly sliced into 2-inch-long strips

1 medium yellow bell pepper, thinly sliced into 2-inch-long strips

2 medium jalapeños, thinly sliced into ⅛-inch rings

Marinade

3 cups vegetable oil

⅓ cup extra-virgin olive oil

⅓ cup unseasoned rice vinegar

2 large cloves garlic, chopped

2 teaspoons coriander seeds

2 tablespoons fresh thyme leaves

¾ teaspoon crushed red pepper flakes, or to taste

1. For the brined vegetables, combine 2 quarts water, salt, and rice vinegar in a large bowl. Add all vegetables and cover with plastic wrap. Set aside to marinate overnight or up to 24 hours at cool room temperature. (If your kitchen is warm, refrigerate.)

2. To make the giardiniera, strain and rinse the brined vegetables under cold running water. Transfer to a large, nonreactive bowl or two large food-storage bags (if you have limited refrigerator space, the latter works well). In another bowl, combine vegetable and olive oils, rice vinegar, garlic, coriander seeds, thyme, and chile flakes. Pour marinade over vegetables and refrigerate for 3 days to allow flavors to develop. Refrigerate vegetables, completely submerged in marinade, for 2 to 3 weeks.

INDEX

DANKE

This book is dedicated to my loyal and supportive customers.

And I must say *vielen dank* to the following people who have enriched my life and made my career so meaningful:

To Colleen Bates and Patty O'Sullivan for believing in this book and the message behind it.

To Jenn Garbee and Wolfgang Gussmack for their tireless work—testing, retesting, writing, and rewriting—and to Albert Hillebrand, whose baking expertise helped their process. This book would not have happened without you.

To Staci Valentine and Valerie Aikman-Smith for contributing their impeccable sense of style.

To California, which not only has provided me with the most incredible produce and fruit, but also a home where I could be myself.

To my grown children, Gina, Roxy, and Hansi, who have challenged me to be a better person.

To my German family—my sister, Susie, her husband, Hans Dieter, my mother, Brunhilde, and father, Karl—to whom I owe my toughness, my work ethic, and my love of bread.

To my Korean in-laws, Susy, José, Jacquie, and Jimmy, who introduced kimchee, ddokbokkee, and japchae into my regular diet.

To my loyal and wonderful friends—Defne, Jamie & Chris, Alex & Jodie, Marcia, Robert, Dale, Gordon, Dana, Ralf & Cordula, Maria, Markus, Allison & Jim, Erla & Trygvvi, and Josiah & Diane—who have supported, encouraged, and cheered me on through all the openings, closures, anniversaries, and milestones. In a notoriously fickle business, it is friends and family who make the high points sweeter and the low points more bearable. Mine are the best.

To Mimi Sheraton, the award-winning food journalist and former *New York Times* critic, who has a deep appreciation and knowledge of German cuisine and has done more to champion it and educate American diners about it than any other writer I know.

To Ruth Reichl, who as the food critic for the *Los Angeles Times* first put me on the map, and to Caroline Bates, who as a writer for *Gourmet* frequently included my work alongside the work of other chefs I admired and respected.

To the California chefs and food lovers who challenge me to up my game and try new things.

To my business team—Pat, Royce, Glen, Seth, and Mendi—who come to my rescue and keep me organized.

To my hardworking and committed staff, who over the years have made and served thousands of pretzel burgers, baked an insane number of breads, pastries, and cakes, and processed thousands of invoices, customer calls, and orders. I could not do it without you.

And most of all, to my business and life partner, my confidante, my tennis rival, my rock, my love, my soulmate, my wife—Patti. I would not be half the person I am today without her.

Published by Prospect Park Books
2359 Lincoln Avenue
Altadena, California 91001
www.prospectparkbooks.com

Distributed by Consortium Books Sales & Distribution
www.cbsd.com

Library of Congress Cataloging in Publication Data
Röckenwagner, Hans.
Das cookbook : German cooking, California style / by Hans Röckenwagner with
Jenn Garbee & Wolfgang Gussmack; photographs by Staci Valentine.
pages cm
In English.
Summary: "Classic German recipes lightened and brightened by an acclaimed Los
Angeles chef"-- Provided by publisher.
ISBN 978-1-938849-33-6 (hardback)
1. Cooking, German. 2. Cooking, American--California style. I. Title.
TX721.R57 2014
641.5943--dc23
2014024385

Recipe development by Wolfgang Gussmack
Recipe testing & writing by Jenn Garbee
Edited by Colleen Dunn Bates
Assistant editor Sascha Bos
Proofread by Patricia Jalbert-Levine
Editorial assistance from Jennifer Bastien

Photography by Staci Valentine
Food and prop styling by Valerie Aikman-Smith
Designed by Anna Goldstein

First edition, second printing

Printed in Canada by Friesens on sustainably produced, FSC®-certified paper